Letters Home

A Drama

by Rose Leiman Goldemberg

A SAMUEL FRENCH ACTING EDITION

SAMUEL FRENCH
FOUNDED 1830
New York Hollywood London Toronto
SAMUELFRENCH.COM

Copyright © 1979, 1980 by Rose Leiman Goldemberg

ALL RIGHTS RESERVED

CAUTION: Professionals and amateurs are hereby warned that *LETTERS HOME* is subject to a Licensing Fee. It is fully protected under the copyright laws of the United States of America, the British Commonwealth, including Canada, and all other countries of the Copyright Union. All rights, including professional, amateur, motion picture, recitation, lecturing, public reading, radio broadcasting, television and the rights of translation into foreign languages are strictly reserved. In its present form the play is dedicated to the reading public only.

The amateur live stage performance rights to *LETTERS HOME* are controlled exclusively by Samuel French, Inc., and licensing arrangements and performance licenses must be secured well in advance of presentation. PLEASE NOTE that amateur Licensing Fees are set upon application in accordance with your producing circumstances. When applying for a licensing quotation and a performance license please give us the number of performances intended, dates of production, your seating capacity and admission fee. Licensing Fees are payable one week before the opening performance of the play to Samuel French, Inc., at 45 W. 25th Street, New York, NY 10010.

Licensing Fee of the required amount must be paid whether the play is presented for charity or gain and whether or not admission is charged.

Stock licensing fees quoted upon application to Samuel French, Inc.

For all other rights than those stipulated above, apply to: Paradigm LA, 360 Park Ave South, 16th Floor, New York, NY, 10010.

Particular emphasis is laid on the question of amateur or professional readings, permission and terms for which must be secured in writing from Samuel French, Inc.

Copying from this book in whole or in part is strictly forbidden by law, and the right of performance is not transferable.

Whenever the play is produced the following notice must appear on all programs, printing and advertising for the play: "Produced by special arrangement with Samuel French, Inc."

Due authorship credit must be given on all programs, printing and advertising for the play.

No one shall commit or authorize any act or omission by which the copyright of, or the right to copyright, this play may be impaired.
No one shall make any changes in this play for the purpose of production.
Publication of this play does not imply availability for performance. Both amateurs and professionals considering a production are strongly advised in their own interests to apply to Samuel French, Inc., for written permission before starting rehearsals, advertising, or booking a theatre.
No part of this book may be reproduced, stored in a retrieval system, or transmitted in any form, by any means, now known or yet to be invented, including mechanical, electronic, photocopying, recording, videotaping, or otherwise, without the prior written permission of the publisher.

ISBN 978-0-573-63018-7   Printed in U.S.A.   #14072

THE AMERICAN PLACE THEATRE

WYNN HANDMAN
DIRECTOR

JULIA MILES
ASSOCIATE DIRECTOR

PRESENTS

LETTERS HOME

by

ROSE LEIMAN GOLDEMBERG

BASED ON SYLVIA PLATH'S "LETTERS HOME"
EDITED BY AURELIA PLATH

Directed by

DOROTHY SILVER

Set by	*Lighting by*	*Costumes by*
HENRY MILLMAN	**ROGER MORGAN**	**SUSAN DENISON**

C A S T
(In Order of Appearance)

AURELIA . . . . DORIS BELACK
SYLVIA . . . . MARY McDONNELL

Production Stage Manager: **MARY R. LOCKHART**

PRESENTED IN ASSOCIATION WITH ROSE LEIMAN GOLDEMBERG
ORIGINALLY PRODUCED BY THE WOMEN'S PROJECT AT
THE AMERICAN PLACE THEATRE

There will be one intermission

THE BAR IN THE SUB-PLOT IS OPEN AT INTERMISSION
There is no smoking in the theatre.
The taking of photographs or recording is strictly prohibited.

AUTHOR'S NOTE

Sylvia Plath was already recognized as a brilliant poet when she took her own life, at thirty, in 1963. Since that tragedy, and in part because of it, the interest in the details of Sylvia's life and death has kept pace with the growing interest in her work. But few biographers have bothered to consult the person who knew Sylvia best and longest. In 1975, in an effort to set the record straight, Aurelia Plath published a huge volume of her daughter's letters home, with spare but meaningful commentary. Every word of the play was drawn from that book. It seemed crucial to me that the real words of this mother and daughter be heard because so much fiction had been written about them. All letters, all dialogue, all words are masks, so the limitations of using the words of the book were only of degree. LETTERS HOME was not a reading; it was performed fully, acting out events as they were told. Actors and director must constantly explore, and finally pinpoint: What exactly is happening at each moment? When that was done with clarity, the whole leaped to life. LETTERS HOME is really two plays: one takes place in the mind of Aurelia: Sylvia's life and their fight to save it. The other takes place here and now, in this audience, as Aurelia, in telling and remembering her story, struggles for and achieves understanding: she is alive and her brilliant child, who needed—and had—her love, is gone. In its first production, we looked for the details of the lives of the two women, and found that they were often together when apart, and apart when together, and so we let them range in and out of each other's "space." They were where Aurelia remembered them, or wanted them to be, for the interior play (the Sylvia play) is in Aurelia's mind. The play is always a dialogue: Aurelia always hears Sylvia; Sylvia is always aware of Aurelia. This merging and separating of the two women is deep in the form of LETTERS HOME, and must be talked about and worked on in rehearsal. They speak the same words, but with different meanings; they do the same actions, often with different intent. They were one and different, as all parents and children, all lovers, are. Humor is essential to the play. All the recognitions of "how it is" between parent and child must be offered to the audience so they can laugh. The more they share this laughter, the more powerful the play becomes, and the more Aurelia can share in gratitude and relief her feelings about her daughter. In the "duets" it is not intended that the audience hear every word of each actor. These are chords sometimes, solos with accompaniment sometimes, rounds sometimes. The levels must be carefully worked on, the legatos must be smooth, the tempos exact. As in any music, the instruments must play responsively together. In its first production, as a workshop at The American Place Theater, LETTERS HOME was performed on a tiny stage divided into three areas. Aurelia's space had a couch, pillows and end tables. Sylvia's space had a desk, books and writing materials. These two were bridged by an open bookcase that Sylvia could "disappear" behind. There was a third small downstage area where Aurelia addressed the audience directly.

Many props helped the actors to establish time and place and to underline the relentless, caged activity of their lives—sweaters to button and unbutton, books, papers, baby clothes, pillows to pat and rearrange, and of course letters. The overriding image of the production was of two women in a cage, moving, talking, trying to act, but trapped, powerless. In the British production of LETTERS HOME, which opened in London to extraordinary rave reviews, the production was much simpler: two areas again, each with a desk, one for Aurelia, one for Sylvia. Very little in the way of props or furniture was used, or needed. The image of the play was of two women living side by side, together and apart. The lives were created simply, but as powerfully as in the New York production. When LETTERS HOME toured, and each local theater supplied the necessary furniture and props, the production was even more simple. And in Melbourne, Australia, twelve thousand miles from Sylvia's life, and death, the director chose to use a simple area and one prop in each act: first an ordinary lawn chair which became, in the actors' hands, a chair, a bed, a hospital stretcher and the space beneath the stairs where Sylvia nearly died—and later a suitcase full of clothes, which, in the final moments of the play, held the clothes that Sylvia used to stop up the doors and windows of her life. In each production the director and the actors found ways to make the play come alive—and each way worked. I hope that in each staging of LETTERS HOME, new actors and directors will find new ways that work for them. LETTERS HOME owes more than most plays to the imagination and devotion of its first director, Dorothy Silver, and to the actors who so brilliantly originated the roles, Doris Belack and Mary McDonnell. But most of all LETTERS HOME is indebted for its very life to the courage, dignity, and strength of Aurelia and Sylvia Plath.

LETTERS HOME

Act I

(*A light picks out Aurelia. She moves forward uncertainly. She is an amateur, in a strange place. Who are these people? What will they think of her?*)

AURELIA. (*To the audience, uncertain.*) My first thanks go to my son Warren J. Plath, and his wife Margaret, whose approval, moral support, and assistance encouraged me to undertake this project. Deep gratitude is owed to each member of my understanding, loyal family. I am deeply grateful to Ted Hughes for generously giving me the copyright for this selection from Sylvia Plath's letters. This book is dedicated to my grandchildren: Frieda and Nicholas, Jennifer and Susan.

(*It means: "I am a woman who above all knows never to forget her children."*)

(*At the mention of* SYLVIA'*s children, Frieda and Nicholas,* SYLVIA *is there.*)

AURELIA. (*With more assurance.*) It may seem extraordinary that someone who died when she was only thirty years old left behind six hundred and ninety-six letters, written to her family between the beginning of her college years in 1950 and her death, early in February 1963. We could not afford long-distance telephoning though, and Sylvia loved to write.

SYLVIA. (*Softly.*) Dearest Mummy, Well, only five minutes till midnight, so I thought I'd spend them writing my first letter to my favorite person. If my printing's crooked, it's only because I drank too much apple cider tonight! (*She laughs.*) Dear Mummy, The most utterly divine thing has happened to me! Dear Mother, Just got your Sunday letter this morning, so I thought I'd drop you a line. Your letters are utterly fascinating and they mean so much. Dear Mum . . . Love, Sivvy.

AURELIA. Throughout these years I had the dream of one day handing Sylvia the huge packet of letters. I felt she could make use of them in stories, and through them, *meet* herself.

SYLVIA. God, today is lovely! My cold is still runny, but with plenty of sleep and nosedrops. . . . By the way, do you suck those buffered penicillins, or swallow with water? I don't want to kill myself!

(*A dark note.* AURELIA *doesn't miss it.*)

Cheerio! Sivvy.

AURELIA. She could taste again the moments of joy and triumph, of sorrow and fear. . . .

SYLVIA. Just to think I'm almost 18! . . . life slipping through my fingers like water. . . . Little time to stop running . . . have to keep on like the White Queen to stay in the same place. Can you make any sense out of this? Maybe you can analyze the ramblings of your child better than she can herself.

AURELIA. Throughout her prose and poetry, Sylvia fused parts of my life with hers. So I feel it is important to lead into an account of her early years by first describing my own. As is often the case in a family having European roots (ours were Austrian), my father made the important decisions during my childhood. However, in the early 1920's financial catastrophe overtook our family.

SYLVIA. (*Softly.*) Dear . . .

AURELIA. My father, broken in spirit and blaming himself most unjustly for his very human error . . .

SYLVIA. (*Softly.*) Dear . . .

AURELIA. handed over the reins of management to my mother.

SYLVIA. (*Overlap.*) Mummy.
AURELIA. Although my father spoke four languages, he and my mother spoke German at home. I too spoke only German. How isolated I felt at recess as I stood by myself in a corner—listening to the other children shouting, "Shut Up!"
SYLVIA. The wave of homesickness hit when I walked into my room, empty and bare. Gosh, I felt lonely!
AURELIA. When I went home at the end of the school day and met my father, I answered his greeting proudly with, "Shut Up!" His face reddened. He took me across his knee and spanked me. Weeping loudly, I sobbed out, "Papa, was bedeutet das?" *What does that mean?*
SYLVIA. So much work I should have done, and my schedule looked so bleak and unsurmountable . . .
AURELIA. He realized I had not understood what the words meant . . .
SYLVIA. I have now snapped out of my great depression—the first real sad mood I've had since I've been here.
AURELIA. He was sorry, hugged me, and asked me to forgive him.
SYLVIA. Now I come to the most thrilling part! . . .
AURELIA. From that time on we spoke English at home. Father was our teacher, and mother and I studied together.
SYLVIA. Whom should my eight hundred fifty dollars come from but Olive Higgins Prouty! Good heavens, she is responsible for all this! (SYLVIA *steps toward* AURELIA, *holds out her hands.*) It is an Indian summer day—blue skied, leaves golden, falling. So I sit here, sheltered, the sun warming me inside. And life is good. Out of misery comes joy, clear and sweet. I feel that I am learning. (AURELIA *takes her hands—their first touch.*)
AURELIA. (*Close now, like girl friends.*) In my junior year in high school, the world of American and English prose and poetry burst upon me, filling me with the urgency to read, read! I lived in a dream world . . .
SYLVIA. I'm being stretched, pulled to heights and depths of thought I never dreamed possible.
AURELIA. . . . a book tucked under every mattress, a book in the bathroom hamper. "What's RiRi doing? Oh, she's reading again."
SYLVIA. If only I can weld the *now* into art and writing later on! . . . like animals storing up fat and then, in hibernation or relaxation, using it up.
AURELIA. I completely identified with the characters in a poem or story.
SYLVIA. If only I'm good enough to deserve all this!
AURELIA. My evergrowing wish became to open to other young people this wonder—to teach.
SYLVIA. I just can't stand the idea of being mediocre?
AURELIA. It was the beginning of my dream for the ideal education of the children I hoped to have some day.
SYLVIA. The question is, shall I plan for a career (I hate the word!) or should I major in English and Art?
AURELIA. Fortunately my mother was most sympathetic, and read my literature books too, saying cheerily
SYLVIA and AURELIA. (*Different tones.*) "More than one person can get a college education on one tuition."
AURELIA. I remembered that vividly when *my* daughter went to Smith.
SYLVIA. You are listening to the most busy and happy girl in the world! I have just been elected to Alpha Phi Kappa Psi, which is the Phi Beta Kappa of the Arts. Also I think I will get at least one sonnet published in the erudite Smith Review this fall. None other than W. H. Auden, the famous modern poet, is to come to Smith next year. (Imagine saying "Oh, yes, I studied writing under Auden!") Your happy girl, Sivvy.
AURELIA. In 1929, after teaching English for the year following my graduation, I decided I would return to the university to earn a Master of Arts degree. Dr. Otto Emil Plath taught the course in Middle High German.

ACT I LETTERS HOME 7

SYLVIA. (*At the mention of Otto: a darker note.*) This is a period of sterility emotionally.
AURELIA. I had met Professor Plath briefly, a very fine-looking gentleman with extraordinarily vivid blue eyes.
SYLVIA. . . . blue skied, leaves golden . . .
AURELIA. I remember the last day of classes at the university very clearly. When I went to say good-bye, Professor Plath played about with a pen on his desk for a bit. Professor Haskell and his wife had invited him to spend the next weekend at their farm. Should I care to join him, he would appreciate it.
SYLVIA. (*Withdrawing.*) My date last night . . . looked rather old.
AURELIA. I learned much about Otto Plath that weekend.
SYLVIA. I feel that I'm cut off from all mankind . . .
AURELIA. He astounded me by telling me that he had married over fourteen years before.
SYLVIA. I don't even know how I can last one week!
AURELIA. He and his wife had soon separated.
SYLVIA. I feel like putting my head on your shoulder and weeping from sheer homesickness.
AURELIA. Were he to form a serious relationship with a young woman now, he would obtain a divorce.

AURELIA.   (*They speak simultaneously.*)   SYLVIA.
He thought my thesis proved we had much in   My face is a mess, all broken out; my tan is fad-
common and he said he would like to know me   ed, my eyes are sunken . . .
better.

SYLVIA. If I could be pretty, I wouldn't mind so much! Boys are strictly secondary in my present life. I find myself numb as far as feeling goes. All I'm trying to do is keep my head above water, and emotions are more or less absent or dormant for the while. It's a good thing to have one less distraction. (*It means: I would not do as you have done.*)
AURELIA. Our friendship developed and deepened. We dreamed of projects jointly shared, involving nature study, travel, writing.
SYLVIA. Life looks so bright when you're rested and well.
AURELIA. I enjoyed teaching until January 1932 when Otto and I were married in Carson City, Nevada.

SYLVIA. Your bewildered, Sivvy.

Then I yielded to my husband's wish that I become a full-time homemaker.
SYLVIA. Dear Mother, I was up in my room talking with a lovely girl (she's one of the people I really can tell things to)—
(*This hurts* AURELIA; SYLVIA *rattles on:*)
—expounding on the misery and inferior feeling of being dateless this weekend. Bill asked me out, but I refused—he just isn't my sort, no spark—when the phone rang. It was Louise. Three boys had just dropped over and would I go out tonight. So I threw on my clothes, all the time ranting on how never to commit suicide, because something always happens! Turned out that my date was a *doll*. I now feel terrific! What a man can do! Love, Sivvy.
AURELIA. (*Seriously.*) As soon as I was certain I was pregnant, I began reading books related to the rearing of children. I was totally imbued with the desire to be a good wife and mother.
(*Bookish* AURELIA! SYLVIA *laughs.*)
SYLVIA. What a man can do!
AURELIA. I quietly followed the "demand feeding" accepted as modern today and labeled old-fashioned in the 1930's. Both my babies were rocked, cuddled, sung to, recited to, and picked up when they cried!
SYLVIA. (*Soft irony.*) Dear Mom
AURELIA. Sylvia was born October 27, 1932, a healthy, eight-and-a-half-pound baby. At luncheon that day, her father told his colleagues, "I hope for one more thing in life—a son, two and a

half years from now." Warren was born April 27, 1935, only two hours off schedule, and *Otto was greeted by his colleagues as " the man who get what he wants when he wants it."*

SYLVIA. I have been rather worried about a friend of mine.
AURELIA. Social life was almost nil for us as a married couple.
SYLVIA. Dear Mummy,
AURELIA. My dreams of "open house" . . .
SYLVIA. My physical exam . . .
AURELIA. for students and the faculty . . .
SYLVIA. consisted in getting swathed in a sheet and passing from one room to another . . .
AURELIA. were not realized.
SYLVIA. in nudity!
AURELIA. All had to be given up for THE BOOK, a treatise on "Insect Societies."
SYLVIA. My height is 5'9" . . .
AURELIA. We worked together on this . . .
SYLVIA. my weight is 137 pounds.
AURELIA. I did the reading and note-taking . . .
SYLVIA. I took such pains . . .
AURELIA. he rewriting and adding his notes.
SYLVIA. to get my ears and heels in a straight line . . .
AURELIA. Then he handed the manuscript to me to put into final form.
SYLVIA. that I forgot to tilt up straight. The result was, "You have good alignment, but you are in constant danger of falling on your face!"
AURELIA. Otto insisted on handling all finances, even to the purchasing of meat, fish and vegetables. The age difference between us, Otto's superior education, his long years of living in college dormitories or rooming by himself, all led to an attitude of "rightful dominance" on his part. At the end of my first year of marriage, I realized that if I wanted a peaceful home, and I did, I would simply have to become more submissive, although it was not my nature to be so.
SYLVIA. Physically, I want a *colossus*! Mentally, I want a man who isn't jealous of my creativity in other fields than children. Graduate school and travel abroad are not going to be stymied by any squalling, breastfed brats. I've controlled my sex judiciously, and you don't have to worry about me at all. The consequences of love affairs would stop me from my independent freedom of creative activity, and *I don't intend to be stopped.* Love, Sivvy.

(AURELIA *nods. She understands. A moment, then:*)

AURELIA. The year after Warren's birth, Otto began to draw more and more into himself.

SYLVIA. Dear Mother, I have been rather worried about a friend of mine. . .

(*A duet now,* AURELIA *leading.*)

AURELIA. He was losing weight, was continually weary, and easily upset by trifles.

SYLVIA. Her usual gaiety has been getting brighter and more artificial as the days go by.

He steadily refused a physician, pushing aside all such suggestions from me, my family, and his colleagues.

SYLVIA. So yesterday, after lunch, I made her come up to my room. At first, she was very light and evasive, but at last her face gave way and melted.

AURELIA. He told me he had diagnosed his own case and that he would *never* submit to surgery.

SYLVIA. It seems that since Thanksgiving she hasn't been able to do her work, and now she can only reiterate, "I can *never* do it, *never.*"

I understood the significance of what he said, for he had recently lost a friend who had succumbed after several operations, to . . .

. . . lung cancer!

I even telephoned my family doctor in Winthrop.

I sensed Otto's unspoken diaganosis: lung cancer.

From this time on . . .

AURELIA. . . . it was heartbreaking to watch a once-handsome, powerfully built man lose his vigor and deteriorate physically and emotionally.

Appealing to him to get medical diagnosis and help only brought on explosive outbursts of anger.

AURELIA. One morning in mid-August, 1940, Otto stubbed his little toe against the base of his bureau. That afternoon I asked to see his foot. The toes were black, and red streaks ran up his ankle. There was no protest this time as I rushed to telephone my doctor. "Diabetes mellitus." The announcement burst upon me like a clap of thunder. So this was his illness, not cancer at all, but an illness which, treated in time, could be lived with and controlled!
From that day on life was an alternation of hope and fear.

On the nurse's first day off, Otto suggested that I get out into the sun with Sylvia. She and I ran along the beach together for only about a half hour. On my return, I found Otto collapsed on the staircase. Somehow I half dragged, half carried him to his bed. (It was a Wednesday, the doctor could not be reached!) I gave Otto his in-

She hasn't been getting enough sleep . . .

. . . but has been waking up early in the mornings, obsessed by the feeling she has to do her work, even if she can only go through the motions, that if she could do the work, nothing would matter.

But her parents were either deceiving her into thinking she was creative or really didn't know how incapable she was. I got scared when she told me how she had been saving sleeping pills and razor blades.

Oh, mother, you don't know how inadequate I felt!

I talked to her all afternoon. I have been thinking of writing a note to her parents, telling them a bit of how tired she is and how she needs rest.

For her mother kept telling her she was foolish and could do it all.

But her mother couldn't really see how incapable the poor girl is of thinking in this state.

SYLVIA. Maybe it's none of my business but I love the girl and feel very inadequate and responsible.
(*Directly to* AURELIA *now:*)

. . . *Inadequate* . . .

. . . *and responsible* . . .

sulin injection; he was so exhausted. In the middle of the night he called me, feverish, shaking from head to foot with chills, bed clothes soaked with perspiration. All the rest of that night I kept changing sheets, sponging his face, holding his trembling hands. As tears streamed down my face, I could only think, "All this needn't have happened; it needn't have happened!"

SYLVIA. If *you* were her mother, she would be all right.

AURELIA. The next day the doctor came. Amputation from the thigh of the gangrened foot and leg would be necessary to save Otto's life. As I handed Dr. Loder his hat, he murmured, "How could such a brilliant man be so *stupid*!"

SYLVIA. If *you* were her mother. If you were . . .

AURELIA. (*With gathering speed.*) On October 12, the amputation was performed. On November 5, when I left Otto his condition was serious. My telephone was ringing when I returned home. It was Dr. Loder. An embolus had struck in a lung and caused my husband's death as he slept.

SYLVIA. If *you* were her mother she would be all right (AURELIA *nods; she understands the accusation.*)

I waited until the next morning to tell the children. When Warren awoke, I told him as quietly as I could that Daddy's sufferings had ended. Warren sat up, hugged me tightly. "Oh, Mummy, I'm so glad *you* are young and healthy!"

Then I faced the more difficult task, telling Sylvia, who was already reading in her bed. She looked at me sternly for a moment, then said woodenly, "I'll never speak to God again!"

SYLVIA. Inadequate. Responsible.

(*On* AURELIA'S *"looked at me,"* SYLVIA *turns away.*)

SYLVIA. (*Wild.*) "I'll never speak to God again!"

SYLVIA. (*Wooden.*) There is the sort of person who has problems and never tells them to anyone, there is the sort of person who has problems and tells them to one understanding person, and there is the sort of person who fools everyone, *even herself*, into thinking there are no problems, except those shallow material ones which can be overcome.

(*On "even herself"* SYLVIA *turns directly to* AURELIA.)

AURELIA. (*Slowly, distinctly.*) I told her that she did not need to attend school that day if she'd rather stay at home. From under the blanket which she had pulled over her head came her muffled voice, "I *want* to go to school."

SYLVIA. (*Remembering.*) "I want to go to school!"

SYLVIA. (*Then, an apology:*) For all my brave, bold talk of being self-sufficient, I realize now how much you mean to me—you and Warren and my dear Grampy and Grammy! I am glad the rain's coming down hard. It's the way I feel inside. I love you so.

AURELIA. After school, she came to me, red-eyed, and handed me a piece of paper. In shaky printing stood these words: I PROMISE NEVER TO MARRY AGAIN. I signed at once.

SYLVIA. (*An explanation.*) I love you so!

SYLVIA. (*Irony.*) What a superlative mother you have been to me!

AURELIA. I looked at the rumpled "document" I had just signed, and *knew* that unless I should have the opportunity to marry a man I respected, loved, and trusted to be a good father to my children, and whom the children wanted for their father, I never *would* marry again.

SYLVIA. I wonder if *I* will ever meet a congenial boy.

AURELIA. This was the explanation I gave Sylvia, as a college student. "That document never kept you from marrying again, did it?" . . . I assured her that it had not.

SYLVIA. (*Quickly.*) All this leads up to my date last night. I told him how I like to write and draw and know people more than just on the surface. He was rather overwhelmed by the fact that I could be so intelligent and yet not be *ugly* or something! This weekend I went out Saturday with Bill. I will ask for Mondays off, because there is nothing I'd rather do than see Dick. Love, love, love, Sivvy.

AURELIA. "Love, love, love . . ." When I viewed Otto at the funeral parlor, he bore no resemblance to the husband I knew, but looked like a fashionable store manikin. The children would never recognize their father, I felt, so I did not take them to the funeral. What I intended as an exercise in courage, for the sake of my children, was interpreted years later by my daughter as "indifference". "My mother never had time to mourn my father's death." (*A deep hurt. She shrugs it off, goes on.*) My husband had no pension. His five thousand dollar life insurance had to be used to pay his medical and funeral expenses. In the summer of 1942, I was invited by the dean of Boston University to develop a course in Medical Secretarial Procedures. At the small salary of eighteen hundred dollars a year, it was providential.

SYLVIA. I don't want you to worry about things, Mummy. I am learning a lot. Now that the hardest twenty years of your life are over you deserve all the returns you can get. P.S. I *will* grow up in jerks, it seems, so don't feel my growing pains so vicariously, dear!

(*It is an apology, and* AURELIA *accepts it with joy.*)

AURELIA. All the girls at Haven House were invited to Maureen Buckley's coming-out party!

SYLVIA. Dear Mother, How can I ever, ever tell you what a unique, dreamlike and astounding weekend I had! Saturday afternoon, at two p.m., about fifteen girls from Smith started out for Sharon, Connecticut. Marcia and I drew a cream-colored convertible (with three other girls and a Dartmouth boy). Picture me then in my navy-blue . . .

AURELIA. (*Adding in.*) bolero suit . . .

SYLVIA. and versatile brown coat, snuggled in the back seat of an open car . . .

AURELIA. *Snuggled?*

SYLVIA. whizzing for two sun-colored hours through the hilly Connecticut valley! The foliage was out in full tilt, and the hills of crimson sumac, yellow maples and scarlet oak that revolved past . . .

AURELIA. the late afternoon sun on them . . .

SYLVIA. were almost more than I could bear. At about five p.m. we rolled up the long drive to "The Elms." God! Great lawns,

AURELIA. huge trees on a hill

SYLVIA. with a view of the valley, distant green cow pastures,

AURELIA. orange and yellow leaves . . .

SYLVIA. A caterer's truck was unloading champagne at the back.

AURELIA. *Champagne!*

SYLVIA. We walked through the hall, greeted by a thousand living rooms, period pieces, rare objects of art everywhere. Marcia and I and Joan Strong,

AURELIA. (a lovely girl)

SYLVIA. had the best deal—a big double bed and bath to ourselves. We lay down under a big quilt for an hour in the gray-purple twilight, conjecturing about the exciting
AURELIA. unknown!
SYLVIA. evening fast coming. Joan, Marcia, and I were driven in a great . . .
AURELIA. black . . .
SYLVIA. Cadillac, to the Sharon Inn, where a lovely buffet supper was prepared.
AURELIA. After supper . . .
SYLVIA. another hour of lying down.
AURELIA. Scarlett O'Hara before the ball!
SYLVIA. And then the dressing! Up the stone steps, under the white colonial columns of the Buckley home. Girls in beautiful gowns clustered by the stairs. Everywhere there were swishes of taffeta, satin . . .
AURELIA. silk!
SYLVIA. I looked at Marcia, and we winked at each other. Walking out in the patio, two stories high, with the elm treetops barely visible through the glassed-in roof . . .
AURELIA. Remember Mrs. Jack's patio?
SYLVIA. The same! Vines trailing from a balcony . . .
AURELIA. fountains playing, . . .
SYLVIA. Balloons, Japanese lanterns, tables covered with white linen. A band platform built up for dancing. I stood open-mouthed,
AURELIA. giddy,
SYLVIA. wanting so much to show *you*! If you had seen me! I looked
AURELIA. beautiful!
SYLVIA. Even daughters of millionaires complimented my dress! About nine-thirty we were standing in fluttering feminine groups, waiting for the dancing to begin. I began to wish I had brought a date, wondering if I could compete with all the tall, lovely girls there. Let me tell you, by the end of the evening, I was so glad I hadn't! The whole Senior Class at Yale was there! Maureen's brother is a senior.
AURELIA. (Ten children in the Catholic family, all brilliant, many writers.)
SYLVIA. A lovely tall hook-nosed freshman named Eric cut in. Turned out we both loved English. Back to the floor with Carl,
AURELIA. the philosophy major,
SYLVIA. who asked me to Cornell weekend. I refused.
AURELIA. Nicely!
SYLVIA. Next I had a brief trot with the Editor of the Yale News. No possibilities there! About then the Yale Whiffenpoofs sang.
AURELIA. Now, suddenly . . .
SYLVIA. A lovely grinning dark-haired boy cut in. "Name?" I asked. "*Constantine.*" He was a wonderful dancer, and twirled so all I could see was a great cartwheel of colored lights. Turned out his father was a general in the Russian Caucasus Mountains! I danced steps I never dreamed of and my feet . . .
AURELIA. just
SYLVIA. flew! A tall boy, who claimed his name was "Plato," did the sweetest thing! In the midst of dancing he said, "I have a picture I want to show you." So we
AURELIA. crossed . . .
SYLVIA. through the cool, leaf-covered
AURELIA. patio . . .
SYLVIA. the sound of the
AURELIA. fountain
SYLVIA. dripping, and entered one of the many drawing rooms. Over the fireplace was a Botticelli
AURELIA. Madonna!
SYLVIA. "You remind me of her," he said.

AURELIA. (*It is happening to her now.*) I was really touched!
SYLVIA. Imagine meeting such fascinating, intelligent, versatile people! And saving best to last, my Constantine. He cut in, and we danced . . .
AURELIA. (*Taking the lead, awkwardly, tenderly.*) and danced. Finally
SYLVIA. we were so hot . . .
AURELIA. and breathless
SYLVIA. that we walked out on the lawn. The night was lovely,
AURELIA. stars, trees big and dark—
SYLVIA. so guess what we did—
AURELIA. (*Dancing.*) Strauss waltzes!
SYLVIA. You should have seen us swooping and whirling . . .
AURELIA. over the grass . . .
SYLVIA. with the music from inside
AURELIA. faint and distant . . . Imagine, on a night like that, to have a
SYLVIA. (*Adding in now.*) handsome . . .
AURELIA. perceptive . . .
SYLVIA. male kiss your hand,
AURELIA. tell you . . .
SYLVIA. how
AURELIA. *beautiful* you were! I asked him what
SYLVIA. happened . . .
AURELIA. when a woman got old, and her physical beauty waned, and he said in his lovely
SYLVIA. liquid
AURELIA. voice, "Why she will always be beautiful to the man she married, we hope."
SYLVIA. (*Takes the lead again.*) I asked if I could tell him my favorite poem. I did . . .
AURELIA. and he loved it! Oh,
SYLVIA. if you could have heard the wonderful way he talked,
AURELIA. about life and the world.
SYLVIA. Imagine! I told him teasingly not to suffocate in my long hair and he said,
AURELIA. "What a divine way to die!"
(*Mother and daughter laugh together.*)
SYLVIA. Probably all this sounds absurd and very silly. But I
AURELIA. never
SYLVIA. expressed myself so clearly and lucidly,
AURELIA. never felt
SYLVIA. such warm, sympathetic response. There is a sudden glorying in womanhood, when someone kisses your shoulder and says "You are charming . . .
AURELIA. beautiful . . .
SYLVIA. and most important,
AURELIA. *intelligent!*"
SYLVIA. It was striking five when I fell into bed beside Marcia. I dreamed . . .
AURELIA. exquisite dreams!
SYLVIA. Brunch at Buckley's at one p.m. on a gray, rainy day, the most amazing repast brought in by colored waiters in great copper tureens. Scrambled eggs . . .
AURELIA. sausages . . .
SYLVIA. a sort of white farina . . .
AURELIA. Lord, what luxury! Back here . . .
SYLVIA. I can't face the dead reality. I still lilt and twirl
AURELIA. with Eric, Plato, and my wholly lovely
SYLVIA. Constantine!
AURELIA. under Japanese lanterns,
SYLVIA. and a hundred moons twining in,

AURELIA. dark leaves . . .
SYLVIA. music spilling out and
AURELIA. echoing yet
SYLVIA. inside my head. *To have had you there!*
AURELIA. In spirit!
SYLVIA. To have had you
AURELIA and SYLVIA. *see me!*
SYLVIA. (*A change of tone.*) I've got to work and work! My courses are frightening. I can't keep up with them! See you the 19th.
AURELIA. Love,
SYLVIA. love,
AURELIA. love,
SYLVIA. Sivvy.

(AURELIA *turns to the audience again.*)

AURELIA. These were the days when we still were together enough to enjoy long talks about books, music, paintings, how they made us feel. For we shared a love of words and considered them as a tool to achieve precise expression in describing our emotions, as well as for mutual understanding.
SYLVIA. Dearest-Mother-whom-I-love-better-than-anybody,
AURELIA. Between Sylvia and me there existed . . .
SYLVIA. You are listening to the most busy and happy girl in the world.
AURELIA. as between my own mother and me
SYLVIA. Honestly, Mum, I could just cry with happiness.
AURELIA. a sort of psychic osmosis, which, at times, was very wonderful,
SYLVIA. The world is splitting open at my feet like a ripe, juicy watermelon!
AURELIA. and comforting,
SYLVIA. If only I can work, work, work to justify all my opportunities. Your happy girl, Sivvy.
AURELIA. at other times, an unwelcome invasion of privacy. Understanding this, I learned, as she grew older, not to refer to previous voluntary confidences on her part.
SYLVIA. Today I got a letter confirming my job. I really hope I earn a lot of money.

(*At the mention of money: another color.*)

AURELIA. The Belmont Hotel, Cape Cod June 11, 1952.
SYLVIA. Your amazing telegram . . .
AURELIA. announcing five hundred dollars, Mademoiselle prize for "Sunday at the Mintons',"
SYLVIA. came just as I was scrubbing tables in the shady interior of the Belmont dining room. I was so excited that I screamed and actually threw my arms around the head waitress who no doubt thinks I am rather insane! Anyhow, psychologically, the moment couldn't have been better. I felt tired. Also I just learned, since I am completely inexperienced I am not going to be working in the main dining room, but in the "side hall" where the managers and top hotel brass eat. So, tips will no doubt net much less. I was beginning to worry about money when your telegram came. God! To think "Sunday at the Mintons' " is *one* of *two* prize stories to be put in a big national slick!!!
AURELIA. The first thing I thought of was: Mother can keep her intersession money and buy some pretty clothes and a special trip or something!
SYLVIA. At least *I* get a winter coat and extra special suit out of the Mintons.
AURELIA. Both Sylvia and I were more at ease in *writing* words of appreciation, admiration, and love than in expressing these emotions verbally—and thank goodness, write them to each other we did!
SYLVIA. So it's really looking up around here, not that I don't have to be scared stiff about money.
AURELIA. I held off
SYLVIA. Even if my feet kill me
because,

as she entered her late teens, after this first week, and I drop 20 trays, I will have the beach, boys to bring me beer, sun,

her response to my spoken praise would be,

"Oh, *you* think I'm wonderful (or look lovely)

and young gay companions.

because you're my

What a life!

Love, your crazy old

mother!"

daughter. Sivvy.

June 15, 1952
 AURELIA. (*The beginning of a terrible time.* AURELIA *knows it.*)
Dear Mother, Do write me letters, Mommy, because I am in a very dangerous state of feeling sorry for myself. Just at present, life is awful. I am exhausted, scared, incompetent, unenergetic and generally low in spirits. Working in side hall puts me apart, and I feel completely uprooted and clumsy. But as tempted as I am to be a coward and escape by crawling back home, I have resolved to give it a good month's trial. Don't worry about me, but do send little pellets of advice now and then.
June *17*, 1952 . . .
 SYLVIA. Dear Mum, It's my week's anniversary here, and I am celebrating the beautiful blue day by spending my morning hour on the beach. Needless to say, I am in a little more optimistic mood than when I wrote you. (*She is up and down.*)
 AURELIA. I've got an idea for a story for Seventeen called, of all appropriate things, "Side Hall Girl." (*And* AURELIA *tries to keep her up—*) I even have a heroine named Marley who is, of course,
 SYLVIA. *me!*
 AURELIA. I should be able to sit down in a few days,
 SYLVIA. and send it to *you* to type and get notarized.
 AURELIA. Would I like to win a summer at Breadloaf!
 SYLVIA. (*—and down; a terrible seesaw.*) But that is really a dream, because *boys* usually win those things, and my style needs to mature a lot yet.
 AURELIA. As for sidehall, I figure I deserve a "bad break," what with all my good fortune winning prizes and going to Smith. I just don't care what people think about me as long as I'm always open, nice, and friendly. Love to you all, Sivvy, your Side Hall philosopher.
June 25, 1952 . . .
 SYLVIA. Just a note to let you know I'm still alive. Never, it seems to me, has work worn me out so much. In spite of everything, I still have my good old sense of humor, and manage to laugh a good deal of the time. I have definitely decided to come home August 10. I will have stayed two months, slaved for two hundred dollars, and will need a good month to recuperate physically and mentally. With all my important and demanding school offices, I can't afford to crack up. Now I'm always so tired that I just can't *retain* anything except what kind of eggs people like for breakfast. Well, tell me what you think of my schemes. Your
 AURELIA. *maturing . . .*
 SYLVIA. Sivvy.
(*Now, a roller-coaster "down."*)
 SYLVIA. Brace yourself and take a deep breath—not too nice.
 AURELIA. (*Bewildered.*) God, will I be glad to get home for a few days of rest.
 SYLVIA. I am sorry to have to admit it, but I am in a rather tense emotional and mental state.
 AURELIA. The crux of the matter is my attitude toward life—hinging on my science course.
 SYLVIA. I have practically considered committing suicide to get out of it; it's like having my nose rubbed in my own slime. It just seems that I am running on a purposeless treadmill, behind and paralyzed, dreading every day of the horrible year ahead when I should be revelling! I have

become really frantic; small choices and events seem insurmountable obstacles, the core of life has fallen apart . . .

AURELIA. I wonder why? Why?

SYLVIA. It affects all the rest of my life; I am behind in my Chaucer unit, feeling sterile in creative writing . . . Everyone else is abroad or falling in love with their courses. I feel I have got to escape this or go mad!

AURELIA. I don't even *want* to understand it, which is the worst yet.

SYLVIA. It seems to have no relation to anything in my life. I have wondered, desperately, if I should go to the college psychiatrist,

AURELIA. try to tell her how I feel about it,

SYLVIA. how it is obsessing all my life, paralyzing my action in every other field. Life seems a mockery . . .

AURELIA. I can't go on like this!

SYLVIA. Luckily I haven't gotten sinus yet; that would be another form of escapism. When one feels like leaving college and *killing* oneself over one course . . . ! Every day more and more piles up. I hate formulas, I don't give a *damn* about valences,

AURELIA. artificial atoms and molecules,

SYLVIA. I am letting it ruin my whole life! I am really *afraid* to talk it over with a psychiatrist, because they might make me drop my activities and spend half my time pounding formulas and petty mathematical relationships into my head, when I basically don't want to learn them! To be wasting all this year of my life,

AURELIA. *obsessed* by this course, *paralyzed* by it,

SYLVIA. Oh, Mother—! . . . Life is so black, anyway. Everything is empty, meaningless. How could I ever persuade the college authorities, how could I convince the psychiatrist? My reason is leaving me! Everybody is happy, but this has obsessed me from the day I got here.

AURELIA. (*Frantic.*) I am driven inward, feeling hollow. No rest cure in the infirmary will cure the sickness in me!

SYLVIA. Love, your hollow girl, Sivvy.

(*Then: relief, exasperation, laughter.*)

AURELIA. Dear Mother, Well, the world has a miraculous and wonderful way of working. You plunge to the bottom, and you think that every straw must be the last. Then you break your leg, and the world falls like a delicious apple in your lap! If a hideous snowy winder with midyears and a broken leg is heaven, what will the green young spring be like? How can I bear the joy of it all! Much overflowing love, Your own Sivvy.

SYLVIA. Today I had my too-long hair trimmed just right for a smooth pageboy, and got, for twelve ninety-five, the most classic pair of silver pumps. With my rhinestone earrings and necklace, I should look like a silver princess. God, how I wish I could win the Madamoiselle contest.

AURELIA. I got my two villanelles back from The New Yorker today.

SYLVIA. Got back the Madamoiselle manuscript today. I don't see how I have any sort of a chance if I just write one or two stories and never revise them or streamline them for a particular market. I want to hit The New Yorker in poetry and Ladies' Home Journal in stories and—

AURELIA. Birthday Greetings! My present is following news. Harpers Magazine just graciously accepted three poems for one hundred dollars in all. Mademoiselle sent ten dollars for runner-up in third assignment. Best love to you, Sivvy.

SYLVIA. I dedicate this Harper's triumph to you, my favorite person in the world! Can't you just hear the critics saying, "Oh, yes, she's been published in Harper's"? When I am rich and famous I will hire you for my private secretary and babytender, and pay you scandalously high wages, and take you on monthly jaunts in my own shocking pink yacht!

AURELIA. (*More softly.*) Letter to Warren; written about May 12, 1953.

SYLVIA. You know, as I do, and it is a frightening thing, that mother would actually kill herself for us if we calmly accepted all she wanted to do for us. She is an abnormally altruistic person, and

I have realized lately that we have to fight against her selflessness as we would fight against a deadly disease.

AURELIA. (*Painfully.*) My ambition is to earn enough so that she won't have to work summers in the future.

SYLVIA. After extracting her life blood and care for twenty years, we should start bringing in big dividends of joy for her. Really, you and I have it good. Food, clothes, best schools in the country—our first choices, all sorts of prizes, etc. Just hope the world doesn't blow up and queer it all before we've lived our good hard lives down to the nub.

AURELIA. (*Desperately cheerful; a last chance.*) Telegram to Sylvia from Mademoiselle: Happy to announce you have won a Mademoiselle 1953 Guest Editorship. You must be available from June 1 through June 26. Please wire collect.

SYLVIA. (*Overlap, excited:*) Dearest Progenitor, I've already sent in the names of four writers: J.D. Salinger; Shirley "The Lottery" Jackson; E.B. White of New Yorker fame; and Irwin Shaw. Hope one of those luminaries consents to be—

AURELIA. The two days at home between her last examination at Smith and her departure for New York were crammed with frantic activity, including—

SYLVIA. (*Overlap.*) New York, New York,
June 4, 1953
Dear Mother, So incredibly much has happened so fast! Gardens, alleys, the rumbling Third Ave. El, the UN with a snatch of the East River; at night at my desk a network of lights, the sound of car horns like the sweetest music . . . I love it!

AURELIA. Whooshed up to the sixth floor. Spent morning with other Eds filling out endless forms. Talked with Fiction Editor, Jobs and Futures Editor, fabulous Editor-in-Chief. Afternoon—rewrote poetry squibs. Assignments announced. I'm Managing Ed. At first I was disappointed at not being Fiction Ed, but now I see how all-inclusive my work is—

SYLVIA. I love it!

AURELIA. Affairs scheduled include fashion tours (e.g. John Frederics hats), UN and Herald Trib tours, movie preview, City Center ballet, TV show, dance at St. Regis Roof. Love, Syrilly.

SYLVIA. I sometimes wonder who is me.

AURELIA. I have been very ecstatic, horribly depressed, shocked, elated, enlightened, and enervated. I want to come home and vegetate in peace this coming weekend, with the people I love around me for a change.

SYLVIA. I can't talk about all that has happened this week . . . I am too weary, too dazed. I have, in the space of six days, toured the second largest ad agency in the world, seen television, heard speeches, gotten ptomaine poisoning from crabmeat the agency served us in their "own special test kitchen" and wanted to *die* very badly for a day! Spent an evening in Greenwich Village with the most brilliant, wonderful man in the world . . . who is *tragically* a couple of inches shorter than I! Spent an evening fighting with a wealthy, *unscrupulous*

AURELIA. (*Wonderingly.*) Peruvian delegate to the UN at a Forest Hills tennis club dance—spent Saturday . . .

SYLVIA. in the Yankee Stadium with all the stinking people in the world, watching the Yankees trounce the Tigers, having our pictures taken, getting lost in the subway and seeing

AURELIA. (*Softly in horror.*) deformed men with short arms that curled

AURELIA and SYLVIA. (*Together.*) like pink, boneless snakes

SYLVIA. around a begging cup stagger through the car, thinking to myself all the time that Central Park Zoo was only different in that there were bars on the windows. Oh, God, it is unbelievable to think of all this at once! My mind will split open!

AURELIA. *I love you* a million times more than any of these slick admen, these hucksters, these wealthy beasts who get drunk in foreign accents all the time.

SYLVIA. Seriously, I am more than overjoyed to have been here a month; it is just that I realize how young and inexperienced I am in the ways of the world. Your exhausted, ecstatic, elegiac New Yorker, Sivvy.

AURELIA. My mother and I met a tired, unsmiling Sylvia on her return from her month in New York City. I dreaded telling Sylvia the news that had come that morning: she had not been accepted as a student in Frank O'Connor's short-story writing class. I knew Sylvia would see it as a rejection of her as a competent or even promising writer, despite all the writing honors and previous publications she had to her credit. At this point, success in short-story writing was her ultimate goal, and Sylvia was too demanding of herself.

SYLVIA. (*Bitterly remembering.*) "By the way, Frank O'Connor's class is filled; you'll have to wait for next summer before registering again."

AURELIA. Sylvia's face in the rear-view mirror went white when I told her, and the look of shock and utter despair that passed over it alarmed me.

SYLVIA. (*A new color: cool, ironic.*) Belknap House, McLean Hospital, Belmont, Mass. December 28, 1953
Dear E. I don't know just how widely the news of my little scandal this summer traveled in the newspaper but I received letters from all over the United States, from friends, relations, perfect strangers and religious crack-pots—and I'm not aware of whether you read about my escapade, or whether *you* are aware of my present situation. At any rate, I'm prepared to give you a brief resume of details.

(*A duet, between mother and daughter now, each telling her side.*)

AURELIA. (*Strongly.*) From that point on, *I* was aware of a great change in her; all her usual joie de vivre was absent. My mother tried to reassure me that this was no doubt temporary, a natural reaction to the strains of the last year. There had been no respite at all, so we encouraged her to "just let go and relax." We packed picnics and drove to beaches in New Hampshire and Massachusetts. At home, she would sunbathe, always with a book in hand,

but never reading it.
After days of this, she finally began to talk to me, pouring out an endless stream of self-deprecation, self-accusation. She had no goal, she said. As she couldn't read with comprehension anymore, much less write creatively, what was she going to do with her life? She had injured her friends, "let down" her sponsors—she went on and on.

Sylvia's self-recrimination even extended to reproaching herself for one of the two prize-winning stories in Mademoiselle. She felt it had been unkind to a young friend, one of the two characters in the story.

SYLVIA. I worked all during the hectic month of June (*Then more softly, a jumble of words.*) in the plushy air-conditioned offices of Mademoiselle magazine helping set up the August issue. I came home exhausted, fully prepared to begin my two courses at Harvard Summer School, for which I'd been offered a partial scholarship. *Then things started to happen.* I'd gradually come to realize

SYLVIA. (*On and on.*) that I'd completely wasted my Junior year at Smith by taking a minimum of courses (and the wrong courses at that), by bluffing my way glibly through infrequent papers, skipping by with only three or four exams during the year, reading nothing more meaty than the jokes at the bottom of the

In an effort to pull herself together Sylvia, who had by this time decided not to attempt any courses at Harvard Summer School, felt that some form of scheduled activity would keep her from feeling that the whole summer was being wasted.

Her plan was that I should teach her shorthand for an hour each morning so that she could "get a job to support my writing—if I can ever write again."

One unforgettable morning, I noticed some partially healed gashes on her legs.

Upon my horrified questioning, she replied, "I just wanted to see if I had the guts!" Then she grasped my hand—hers was burning hot to the touch—
and cried passionately, "Oh, Mother, the world is so rotten! I want to die!"

"*Let's die together!*" I took her in my arms, telling her that she was ill, exhausted, that she had everything to live for and that I would see to it that she wanted to. We saw our own doctor within an hour; she recommended psychiatric counseling.

And the long summer of seeking help began. The first psychiatrist:

column in The New Yorker and writing nothing but glib jingles in an attempt to commune with W. H. Auden. I had gaily asserted that I was going to write a thesis on James Joyce (when I hadn't even read Ulysses through thoroughly once!) And take comprehensives in my senior year, when I wasn't even familiar with the most common works of Shakespeare, for God's sake! (*Wilder.*) To top it off, all my friends were either writing novels in Europe, planning to get married next June, or going to med. school. The one or two males I knew were either proving themselves genii in the midst of adversity, or were not in the market for the legal kind of love for a good ten years yet, and were going to see the world and all the femmes fatales in it before becoming victims of wedded bliss.

Anyhow, to sum up my reactions to the immediate problem at hand I decided at the beginning of July to save a few hundred dollars, stay home, write, learn shorthand, and finesse the summer school deal. (*Heavy irony.*) You know, sort of "live cheap and be creative."

Truth was, I'd counted on getting into Frank O'Connor's writing course at Harvard,

(*Low, on and on.*) but it seemed that several thousand other rather brilliant writers did, too, and so I didn't; so I was miffed, and figured if I couldn't write on my own, I wasn't any good anyhow.

It turned out that not only was I totally unable to learn one squiggle of shorthand, but I also had not a damn thing to say in the literary world; because I was sterile, empty, unlived, unwise, and UNREAD. And the more I tried to remedy the situation, the more I became unable to comprehend ONE WORD of our fair old language.

SYLVIA. I began to frequent the offices and couches of the local psychiatrists, who were all

He insisted that a series of shock treatments would be *beneficial.* I felt so inadequate, so alone. A kind neighbor took Sylvia and me to the hospital for the treatments; it was she who sat with me, holding my hand as we waited for Sylvia to reappear, for though I had pleaded to accompany her, I was *not allowed to do so!*

The consultations with the referred psychiatrist, an older man, gentle and fatherly, gave me a ray of hope. He prescribed sleeping tablets, which he told me to administer each night—and which I kept locked in a metal safety case. (*Her voice rising.*) Sylvia still talked to me constantly in the same self-deprecating vein, becoming very agitated at times as she noted the approaching date of the fall term of college.

AURELIA. (*Deeply troubled, reliving it.*)
On August 24, a blisteringly hot day, a friend invited us to a film showing of the coronation of Queen Elizabeth II. Sylvia said she wanted to stay home with her grandparents, but urged me to go.

(AURELIA *looks at* SYLVIA, *who smiles dazzlingly.* She looked particularly well this day; her eyes sparkled, her cheeks were flushed. Nevertheless, I left her with a sense of uneasiness, feeling that her buoyancy was contrived.

I found it difficult to concentrate . . . (*More softly.*) on the slow-moving, archaic ceremony on the screen, and in the middle of it I all at once felt myself

running back and forth on summer vacations. I became unable to sleep; I became immune to increased doses of sleeping pills, I underwent a rather brief and traumatic experience of badly given shock treatments on an outpatient basis.

Pretty soon, the only doubt in my mind was the precise time and method of committing suicide.

(*Low.*) The only alternative I could see was an eternity of hell for the rest of my life in a mental hospital, and I was going to make use of my last ounce of free choice and choose a quick clean ending. I figured that in the long run it would be more merciful and inexpensive to my family; (*Then with great clarity, and passion.*) instead of an indefinite incarceration of a favorite daughter in the cell of a State San, instead of the misery and disillusion of sixty odd years of metal vacuum, of physical squalor I would spare them all by ending everything at the height of my so-called career, while there were still illusions left among my profs, still poems to be published in Harper's, still a memory at least that would be worthwhile.
SYLVIA. (*Same tone as "live cheap and be creative."*) Well, I tried drowning, but that didn't work.

So I hit upon what I figured would be the easiest way out. *When* AURELIA *turns away, the smile fades.*)

I waited until my mother had gone to town. (*Now* SYLVIA *takes the lead.*) my brother was at work, and my grandparents were out in the back yard. Then I broke the lock of my mother's

once found myself filled with terror such as I had never experienced in my life. Cold perspiration poured down me; my heart pounded. I wanted to get out of my seat and rush from the theater. I forced myself to remain quiet until the close, then begged my friend to drive me home at once. Propped against a bowl of flowers on the dining-room table was a note in Sylvia's handwriting: Have gone for a long walk. Will be home tomorrow."
The nightmare of nightmares had begun.

The report of Sylvia's disappearance which I phoned to the police, was issued over the radio. Then I discovered that the lock to my steel case had been broken open and the
bottle of sleeping pills was missing.

At noon on the third day

He dashed from the table. "Call the ambulance!"

He had found his sister, returning to consciousness in the crawl space beneath the downstairs bedroom.

(*Open pain, passion.*) In minutes she was carried into the ambulance, and we followed to the hospital. When I was allowed to see her, there was an angry-looking abrasion under her right eye and considerable swelling. Her first words were a moaned "Oh, no!" When I took her hand and told her how we rejoiced she was alive and how we loved her, she said weakly, "It was my last act of love."

(*They are playing together, cello & violin.*)

As soon as the news of our finding Sylvia was made public, I received a sympathetic telegram from Mrs. Prouty.

safe, took out the bottle of fifty sleeping pills, and descended to the dark sheltered ledge in our basement, after having left a note to my mother that I had gone on a long walk and would not be back for a day or so. I swallowed quantities and blissfully succcumbed to the whirling blackness that I honestly believed was eternal oblivion.

My mother believed my note, sent out searching parties, notified the police, and, finally on the second day or so, began to give up hope when

she found that the pills were missing.

My brother finally heard my weak yells.

a nightmare of flashing lights, strange voices, large needles,

and a *hatred* toward the people who would not let me die—but insisted rather in dragging me back into the hell of sordid and meaningless existence!

SYLVIA. (*An attempt at cool irony again.*) I won't go into the details that involved two sweltering weeks in the Newton-Wellesley Hospital, exposed to the curious eyes of all the student nurses, attendants and passers-by, or the two weeks in the psychiatric ward of the Mass. General, where the enormous open sore on my cheek gradually healed, leaving a miraculously intact eye, plus a large, ugly brown scar under it.

Suffice it to say that by fairy godmother-type maneuverings, my scholarship benefactress at Smith got me into the best mental hospital in

One of Sylvia's deep concerns throughout her illness had been that she had not proven herself worthy of the scholarship help given her.

the U.S., where I had my own attractive private room and my own attractive private psychiatrist. I didn't think improvement was possible. It seems that it is.

I have emerged from insulin shock and electric (ugh!) shock therapy with the discovery, among other things, that I can laugh, if the occasion moves me (and, surprisingly enough, it sometimes does), and get pleasure from sunsets, walks over the golf course, drives through the country. I still miss the old love and ability to enjoy solitude and reading. I need more than anything right now

(AURELIA *turns to her on "love." * SYLVIA *motions her away.*)

what is, of course, most impossible, someone to love me, to be with me at night when I wake up in shuddering horror and fear of the cement tunnels leading down to the shock room, to comfort me with an assurance that no psychiatrist can quite manage to convey. (*Then an attempt at the old gay bravery.*) The worst, I hope, is over.

AURELIA. (*Painfully.*) My dear Mrs. Plath: It is good news to know that your general practitioner finds no trace of psychoses; a neurosis can be long drawn-out and requires even more wise handling. Of course Sylvia doesn't want to see anyone now.

(AURELIA *understands:* SYLVIA *doesn't want to see her.*) It will take some time, you say, for her face injury to heal. (Poor child! I am so sorry!) You have been through a terrific ordeal and I know well you are still terribly anxious and beset by all the decisions to be made and also by Sylvia's suffering.

I can now have visitors, go for drives, supervised walks, and hope to have "ground privileges" by the end of this week,

I wish I could help relieve your anxiety about Sylvia's future, but

freedom to walk about the grounds alone, to frequent the Coffee Shop and the library, as well as the Occupational Therapy rooms.

I am very hopeful there will be no disfiguring scars left on either her body or soul. Sincerely, Olive H. Prouty.

I long to be out in the wide open spaces of the very messy dangerous, real world which I

still love, in spite of everything. (*A blazing false smile.*) As ever. Syl.

(*The two women turn to each other.*)

BLACKOUT

END OF ACT I

ACT II

SYLVIA. Hello again! Where to begin! I feel that I am walking in a dream.

AURELIA. Sylvia returned to Smith in the second semester, taking only three courses.

(*Carefully-They are feeling each other out, reassuring each other—making boundaries.*)

SYLVIA. Needless to say, it is simply wonderful to be back.

AURELIA. She was not on scholarship at this time. I wanted her to be free of any sense of obligation and cashed in an insurance policy to meet her expenses. During the first few months we telephoned frequently—more for my peace of mind than hers.

SYLVIA. I am so happy about my thesis on Dostoevsky, and also rooming with Nancy, who is now my dearest friend. Am still chatting with Dr. Booth, the college psychiatrist, once a week—mostly friendly conversations. I really feel I am an extremely well-adjusted buoyant person, continually happy in a steady fashion, not ricocheting from depths to heights, although I do hit heights now and then. Love, Sivvy.

AURELIA. Sylvia was welcomed back by her classmates and the faculty. Understanding and every possible kindness were given her. She picked up an active "date life," which helped build up confidence, and she said she enjoyed herself "in a casual, hedonistic way."

SYLVIA. I am so happy, so elated! Smith just voted me a scholarship of twelve hundred and fifty dollars!

AURELIA. She made me think of deep-sea plants, the roots firmly grasping a rock, but the plant itself swaying in one direction then another with the varying currents that pass over and around. It was as though she absorbed each new personality she encountered, and tried it on, later to discard it. I kept saying to myself, "This is only a stage; it will pass." Her memory grasped and held to discords and seemed to

SYLVIA. (*Softly, trying out new moods like grace notes.*) You'll be happy to hear of . . . Wonderful letter from . . . See you Saturday . . .

Tomorrow I have . . .
I really feel that . . .

I love . . . I feel.

have lost recollections of shared childhood joys. Kindnesses and loving acts were now viewed cynically, analyzed for underlying motives. Then, periodically, to our relief, her sunny optimism would reassert itself, and we would be once more showered with affection.

SYLVIA. Today I cut because I wrote my first poem—a sonnet—since last May! While I have not got a paying job, I *am* the correspondent to the New York Tribune—good experience, even if it doesn't pay money. Both Sassoon and his roommate claim to be intensely in love with me! I won one poetry prize this year. Also, just got elected president of Alpha Phi Kappa Psi, a very honorary post with a minimum of work and a solid gold, ruby-studded pin from Tiffany's—minor events compared to the splash last year, but events nevertheless. See you in a week.

AURELIA. This, too, was a very turbulent summer. Sylvia returned from Smith with her hair bleached! Although initially shocked, I had to admit, it was becoming.

SYLVIA. It was more than a surface alteration. She was trying out a more daring, adventuresome personality, and one had to stand by and hope that neither she

AURELIA. nor anyone else

SYLVIA. would be deeply hurt.

AURELIA. She strove for

SYLVIA. and achieved

AURELIA. competency in her various undertakings, domestic and scholarly. She would be disarmingly confiding, then withdraw, and I quickly learned that it was unwise to make any reference to the

SYLVIA and AURELIA. *sharing*

AURELIA. that had taken place.

SYLVIA. My main concern in the next year is to grow as much as possible. I need space and solitude. I feel that you will understand. (AURELIA *nods; she is trying to.*)

AURELIA. The ulcer I had developed during my husband's illness had been quiescent until the time of Sylvia's breakdown. In 1954, in an attempt to recover again, I took the summer off and joined my parents in a rented cottage on Cape Cod. Sylvia visited with friends in New York, attended several weddings, then returned to Wellesley to "keep house."

SYLVIA. I do want you to know how I appreciate time for a retreat of sorts here. Of course, the house is lonely without you, but I have to fight for solitude.

AURELIA. Space and solitude. I am happy I dyed my hair back, even if it fades and I have to have it touched up once or twice. I feel that this year I would much rather look demure and discreet.

SYLVIA. Dearest Mother, Now I think it is time for me to concentrate on the hard year ahead, the last push of my senior year. I know that underneath the blazing jaunts in yellow convertibles I am really regrettably conventional, and puritannical, but I needed to practice a certain healthy bohemianism for a while, to swing away from the grayclad, basically dressed, brown-haired, clock-regulated, responsible, salad-eating, water-drinking, bed-going, economical, practical girl I had become—and that's why I needed to associate with people who were very different from myself.

AURELIA. At this time, I was in the Newton-Wellesley Hospital. Sylvia telephoned, telling the nurse, that her news would help me more than anything else could. She had been awarded a Fulbright grant to study at Cambridge University!

SYLVIA. I am so happy, so encouraged! Now, just so you can remember it, I'll give you a list of prizes and writing awards for this year:

AURELIA and SYLVIA. (*Passing it back and forth, overlapping.*)

$ 30. Dylan Thomas honorable mention for "Parallax," Madamoiselle.
$ 30. For cover of novel symposium, Madamoiselle
$ 5. Alumnae Quarterly article on Alfred Kazin
$100. Academy of American Poets Prize (10 poems)
$ 50. Glascock Prize (tie)
$ 40. Ethel Olin Corbin Prize (sonnet)
$ 50. Marjorie Hope Nicholson Prize (tie) for thesis
$ 25. Vogue Prix de Paris (one of 12 winners)
$ 5. Atlantic for "Circus in Three Rings"
$100. Christophers (one of 34 winners)
$ 15. Madamoiselle for "Two Lovers and a Beachcomber by Real Sea"
$470. TOTAL, plus much joy!

SYLVIA. Get well *fast*—can't wait to see you Wednesday. All my love, Sivvy.

AURELIA. I had permission to leave the hospital to attend Sylvia's commencement, and made the trip flat on a mattress in a friend's station wagon. Adlai Stevenson gave the commencement address, Marianne Moore was one of the honorary-degree recipients, and Alfred Kazin waved to Sylvia as she returned from receiving her degree. I was in full accord with her as she later whispered in my ear, "My cup runneth over!"

(*They are one. For a moment. Then:*)

SYLVIA. Dear Warren, I know the Fulbright is the best and only thing for me; staying in New England or even New York would suffocate me completely. . . . It does take guts to change and grow. My wings need to be tried!

AURELIA. September 25, 1955

SYLVIA. Dearest Mother, London is simply fantastic!

AURELIA. Oh, mother, every alleyway is crowded with tradition, and I can feel a peace, reserve, lack of hurry here which has centuries behind it.
SYLVIA. The days are generally gray, with a misty light
AURELIA. and landscapes are green-leaved in
SYLVIA. silver mist
AURELIA. like Constable's paintings.
SYLVIA. I would welcome any cookies!
AURELIA. I have to begin life on *all* fronts again, as I did two years ago, but I have all that experience behind me.
SYLVIA. I can't wait to start meeting the British men!
AURELIA. Don't worry that I will marry some idiot, or even anyone I don't love. I simply couldn't.
SYLVIA. Don't worry that I am a "career woman," either. I am definitely *meant* to be married and have children and a home, and write. If you only knew how hard it is to have so much strength and love to give. I don't know how I can bear to go back to the States unless I am married.
AURELIA. When you think of it, it is so little of our lives we really spend with those we love. . . .
SYLVIA. Met, by the way, a brilliant poet at the wild party last week; will probably never see him again, but wrote my best poem about him afterwards—the only man I've met here who'd be strong enough to be equal with—such is life.
AURELIA. The man was Ted Hughes.
SYLVIA. Oh, mother, if only you knew how I am forging a soul!
AURELIA. The most shattering thing is that I have fallen terribly in love, which can only lead to great hurt.
SYLVIA. The strongest man in the world, ex-Cambridge, brilliant poet, whose work I loved before I met him, a large, hulking, healthy Adam, half-French, half Irish,
AURELIA. with a voice like the thunder of God!—a singer, story-teller, lion and world-wanderer, a vagabond who will never stop. You should see him, hear him!
SYLVIA. He has a health and hugeness. The more he writes poems, the more he writes poems! I am writing poems, and they are better and stronger than anything I have ever done.
AURELIA. I am full of poems; my joy whirls in tongues of words. I have never been so exultant.
SYLVIA. I cook trout on my gas ring and we eat well. We drink sherry in the garden and romp through words. He tells me fairy stories and dreams, marvellous colored dreams, about certain red foxes.
AURELIA. My God,
SYLVIA. this is Eden here, and the people are all shining, and I must show it to you! All my love Your singing girl, Sivvy.
AURELIA. If you have a chance, could you send over my *Joy of Cooking*?
SYLVIA. *You must come to England*! You, alone have had crosses that would cause many a stronger woman to break. You have borne daddy's long hard death, your own ulcer attacks. You have seen me through that black night when the only word I knew was NO and I thought I could never write or think again. You deserve, too, to be with the loved ones who can give you strength. I am waiting for you, and your trip shall be for your own soul's health and growing.
AURELIA. To my complete surprise, three days after landing at Southampton, I found myself the sole family attendant at Sylvia's and Ted's secret wedding. From Paris I saw them off for "a writing honeymoon on a shoestring" in Spain.
SYLVIA. For the first time in my life, mother, I am at peace. For the first time I am free. I feel that all my life, all my pain and work has been for this. I see the power and voice in him that will shake the world alive. Even as he sees into my poems and will work with me to make me a woman poet the world will gape at; even as he sees into my character and will tolerate no fallings away from my best self.
AURELIA. In spring, news that Ted's first book of poetry had been accepted was followed by the welcome announcement that Sylvia had been appointed to teach Freshman English—at Smith!

SYLVIA. My most cherished dream is to bring him home with me next June for a sort of enormous barbeque in Wellesley, to which I will invite all the neighbors, young couples, and dear people like Mrs. Prouty, Dr. B., just to meet him before we set out on our world-wandering—not really wandering, but living and teaching English in country after country, writing, mastering languages and having many, many babies.

AURELIA. I know you're fantastically busy, but have two small desperate requests: could you please possibly send my *Joy of Cooking* and *lots* more 3-cent stamps. I'm starting to send batches of Ted's poems out to American magazines. I want the editors to be crying for him when we come next June.

SYLVIA. He has commissioned me his official agent and writes prolifically as shooting stars in August. I have great faith in his promise; we are coming into our era of richness, both of us, late maturing, reaching beginning ripeness after twenty-five and going to be fabulous old people!

AURELIA. (*Remembering, cautioning.*) "We dreamed of projects jointly shared, involving nature study, travel, writing. . . ."

SYLVIA. We are utterly in love with each other! Mrs. Sylvia Hughes, Mrs. Ted Hughes, Mrs. Edward James Hughes, Mrs. E. J. Hughes, (wife of the internationally known poet and genius), and

AURELIA. "Dr. Otto Emil Plath . . ."

SYLVIA. Dearest, dearest Mother, If only you could see wherever Ted and I go people seem to love us. My whole thought is how to please him. The joy of being a loved and loving woman; that is my song.

AURELIA. Life is work *and* joy.

SYLVIA. The girls at Smith are *unscrupulous*! I would be absurd to throw Ted into such hysterical, girlish adulation. I shouldn't have a minute's peace! . . . I shall apply for Ted at *Amherst*!

AURELIA. Oh, he has everything . . .

SYLVIA. And I am so happy with him! (*More softly.*) I was most moved by your account of S.,

AURELIA. (the son of a dear friend).

SYLVIA. He must feel, as I felt, only three years ago, that there is no way out for him. I wish you could somehow use me as an example. Tell him I went through six months where I literally couldn't read, felt I couldn't take courses at Smith, even the regular program. I am sure he is not that badly off.

AURELIA. Get him to go easy on himself.

SYLVIA. I remember I was terrified that if I wasn't successful writing, no one would find me interesting or valuable. Psychiatrists blither about father and mother relationships when some common sense, stern advice about practical things and simple human intuition can accomplish much. I hope you will adopt him for my sake.

AURELIA. (*Softly.*) When he dies, his marks will not be written on his gravestone. If he has loved a book, been kind to someone, enjoyed a certain color in the sea—that is the thing that will show whether he has lived. Show you love him and demand nothing of him but the least that he can give.

SYLVIA. (*Another color.*) Hello, Hello! It must not yet be 6 a.m. in the hamlet of Wellesley, but I thought you wouldn't mind being wakened by such good news. "*Hawk in the Rain* judged winning volume Poetry Center First Publication." We both jumped about yelling and roaring like mad seals. I am so happy Ted's book is accepted first! Genius will out!

AURELIA. (*Very careful; she will not criticize.*) From the time Sylvia was a very little girl, she catered to the male of any age, to bolster his sense of superiority.

SYLVIA. I can rejoice much more, knowing Ted is ahead of me!

AURELIA. In her diary she described coming in second in the spelling contest. "I am so glad Don won," she wrote. "It is always nice to have a boy be first. And I am second-best speller in the whole Junior High!"

SYLVIA. I have worked so closely on these poems of Ted's and typed them so many times that I feel ecstatic about it all. What a blessing to wear heels with Ted and still be "little!" I've been bogged down on two stories I'm working on for the *Ladies' Home Journal*. Well, he took me on a long walk, listened to me talk the whole plot out, showed me what I'd vaguely felt I should change about the end. Last night he read all 30 pages of it, word for word, unerringly pointing out awkwardness here or an unnecessary paragraph there . . . Doesn't it all sound heavenly and exciting? Work, work, that is the secret, with someone you love more than anything. See you in a week!

AURELIA. Sylvia and Ted arrived in Wellesley the last week in June 1957, and were given a catered reception in a large tent in the rear of our small house, attended by more than seventy people. Sylvia was radiant as she proudly introduced her poet husband. A few days later her brother drove them to a small cottage in Eastham. Here Sylvia prepared her work for the fall semester at Smith College.

SYLVIA. Dearest Warren, My ideal of being a good teacher, writing a book on the side, and being an entertaining homemaker, cook and wife is rapidly evaporating! This is not the life for a writer. I am sacrificing my energy grubbing over sixty-six Hawthorne papers a week in front of a rough class of spoiled bitches! If I knew *how* to teach a short story, or a novel, or a poem, I'd at least have that joy. But I'm making it up as I go along, through trial and error, mostly error.

AURELIA. It's easier for the men, I think.

SYLVIA. It's Ted who really saves me! He is sorry I'm so enmeshed in this and wants me to write starting this June. How I long to write on my own again! When I'm describing Henry James' use of metaphor, I'm dying to be making up my own metaphors. When I hear a professor saying: "Yes, the wood is shady, but it's a *green* shade"—I feel like throwing up my books and writing my own bad poems and bad stories! I don't like talking *about* D. H. Lawrence. I like reading him selfishly for an influence on my own life and my own writing. Ted and I are fermenting plans, hoping to rent a little apartment on the slummy side of Beacon Hill, which we love—work at unresponsible jobs (for money, bread and experience) and *write* for a solid year.

AURELIA. Very few people can understand this!

SYLVIA. There is something suspect, especially in America, about people who don't have ten-year plans, or at least a regular job. We found this out trying to establish credit at a local store. We fitted into none of the form categories of "The Young American Couple." I had a job, Ted didn't; we owned no car, were buying no furniture on the installment plan, had no charge accounts, no TV . . .

AURELIA. When we are both wealthy and famous, our work will justify our lives.

SYLVIA. God feeds the ravens. I hope *you* understand this better than mother!

AURELIA. The following is from a page of my diary, Sunday, August 3, 1958. "We visited Ruth on Thursday. She had come home with her five-day-old son, a wee, red-faced infant. I believe I felt Ted withdraw from him—a very young baby can be so raw and weird looking. Sylvia, however,

SYLVIA. opened the curled hand and stretched out the exquisitely finished little fingers; examined the wrinkled petal of a foot—each toe a dot, yet complete with a speck of pearly nail—the whole foot shorter than her little finger.

AURELIA. There was such warmth, such yearning in Sivvy's face, my heart ached for her."

SYLVIA. Every time you make a choice you have to sacrifice something.

AURELIA. Unlike mother, I am a writer, not a teacher.

SYLVIA. After I have written twenty stories and a book or two of poems, I might be able to keep up writing with work or a family . . .

AURELIA. By spring 1959, both writers had published a number of poems and Ted was awarded a Guggenheim grant. They now planned to have a child, whom Ted wished to be English-born. Sylvia concurred in this decision.

SYLVIA. (*Softly.*) Dear Warren, Ted has . . . Ted and I . . .

AURELIA. On the day they left, Sylvia was wearing her hair in a long braid down her back with a little red wool cap on her head, and looked like a high school student. As the train pulled out, Ted called, "We'll be back in two years!"

SYLVIA. Dear Mother, I have gone through a very homesick and weary period but once we get a foothold in London, life will become much better.

AURELIA. Wonderful news via telegram, for Ted. The Somerset Maugham Award, just over one thousand dollars, to be spent "enlarging his world-view." We envision the Greek Islands next winter, and all sorts of elegant sunsaturated schemes.

SYLVIA. The first British publisher I sent my new collection of poems to, wrote back within the week accepting them! Amaze of amaze! *The Colossus and Other Poems,* by Sylvia Plath.

AURELIA. For Ted . . . Went to my doctor again today, and he let me listen to the baby's heartbeat! I was so excited. I'm going to see if London has diaper service.

SYLVIA. Lots of love from us both.

AURELIA. On the morning of April 1, 1960, at about three a.m., the phone at my bedside rang. "Mother," said a tremulous voice. "Sylvia!" I cried. "Is it Nicholas or Frieda Rebecca?" "Oh, Frieda Rebecca, of course! Ein Wunderkind, Mummy. Ein Wunderkind!"

SYLVIA. From where I sit, propped up in bed, I can see her, pink and healthy, sound asleep. "A wonder child." Of course, of course! Alas, she has my nose! On her, though, it seems quite beautiful.

AURELIA. I have never been so happy in my life!

SYLVIA. Ted was there the whole time. You should see him rocking her and singing to her! She looks so tiny against his shoulder, her four fingers just closing around one of his knuckles. Already she shows a funny independence and temper.

AURELIA. Things seem much calmer and more peaceful with the baby around. Ted will have a study and utter peace by the time I have all my strength back and am coping with baby and household.

SYLVIA. Dear Mother, I've been going through a rather tired spell, at the depressing, painful stage of trying to start writing after long silence.

AURELIA. Something odd happened to me today.

SYLVIA. I was walking the baby, the air too cold and windy to go far, and half-dreamily let my feet carry me down a road I'd never been before. Saw a house for sale, 41 Fitzroy Road, *the street where Yeats lived.* I was so excited that I ran home and called Ted. Well, of course I had visions of a study for Ted in the attic, a study for me, a room for guests (you)—

AURELIA. Ted is much more hesitant than I to commit himself.

SYLVIA. And I am loath to jeopardize

AURELIA. Ted's

SYLVIA. writing. I am thinking of getting a job myself, if

AURELIA. Ted

SYLVIA. would just feed the baby. By the way,

AURELIA. Ted

SYLVIA. has a real desire to take a degree in zoology—a job he could give his heart to, not the fancy literary white-collar work or English teaching which would make him unhappy . . . Any ideas or suggestions? (AURELIA *shrugs; how can she answer that?*) I am now working very hard on women's magazine stories. I also have a fine, lively agent, so after I get acceptances here, they'll send any stuff good enough to the Saturday Evening Post, etc.

AURELIA. I am very excited that children seem to be an impetus to my writing. As soon as I start selling, I could afford a half-day babysitter to do the drudge-work.

SYLVIA. Oh, how I look forward to your coming! My heart lifts now that the year swings toward it. . . . Could you possibly alter your flight to cover August 20? The reason I'm asking is, I discovered today your second grandchild is due about then.

AURELIA. Dearest Mother, I feel awful to write you now after changing your plans and probably telling your friends about another baby, because I lost the little baby this morning, and feel really terrible about it. Ted is taking wonderful care of me. He is the most blessed, kind person in the world. All weekend while I was in the shadow of this, he gave me poems to type and generally distracted me.

SYLVIA. Do write and cheer me up. . . Sivvy.

AURELIA. Actually, the most wonderful thing you could do for us would be to live here with Frieda for two weeks, while we had our first real vacation in France.

SYLVIA. . . . with the Merwins.

AURELIA. By now Ted had the use of a friend's study where he could work in quiet, and Sylvia worked there, too, drafting *The Bell Jar*—unknown to me.

SYLVIA. Dear Mother, I am working fiendishly at the Merwins' study seven mornings a week, as they are coming home at the end of May, and I've a lot I want to finish before then. I have found that the whole clue to happiness is to have four to five hours perfectly free and uninterrupted to write in, the first thing in the morning—no phone, doorbells, or baby.

AURELIA. I'm trying to get the bulk of my writing done before you come, but even if I work in the mornings, we'll have the whole rest of the day together.

SYLVIA. I think you'll be a lot more comfortable at the Merwins'.

AURELIA. (*Nods. She understands.*) In July 1961, I visited them, staying with Frieda while Sylvia and Ted went on a holiday to France. Sylvia was again pregnant, and they were longing to establish a home of their own . . . Dear Warren, On Thursday the two of them took off for Devon, a trip of five hours by car. They have been sending for real estate listings since early spring, and had selected eight places to visit . . .

SYLVIA. all sounding lush!

AURELIA. While they were gone, Frieda decided to cut her twelfth tooth. Neither of us slept much as a result. Well, Sivvy and Ted returned at midnight, Friday,

SYLVIA. exhausted.

AURELIA. Seven of the eight houses were impossible.

SYLVIA. Some actually ruins.

AURELIA. But the third place they saw they fell in love with, and if all is correct legally, I guess they are going to purchase it. It is the ancient

SYLVIA. Yes!

AURELIA. house of Sir and Lady Arundel, who were there to show them about. The Arundels impressed Sivvy and Ted, and seemed anxious to get people who would have a sense of the historic value of the place.

SYLVIA. There is a Roman mound there!

AURELIA. From Sivvy's description, I gathered the following statistics: The main house has

SYLVIA. nine rooms,

AURELIA. A great lawn in front, a thatched roof—

SYLVIA. Honest! And a "cottage" . . .

AURELIA. that is in great need of repair! I wish I could see it, but Ted and Sylvia are glad (I sense) that the distance makes this impossible. They don't mind *your* seeing it, but said that I would find flaws that they intend to eradicate.

SYLVIA. (*Overlap.*) I shall be so happy to start fixing it up!

AURELIA. (*Real concern.*) Both Ted's mother and I are loaning them five hundred pounds so they won't be snowed under by the terrible interest rate . . .

AURELIA. (*It's so much!*) Six and a half per-   SYLVIA. (*It's so little!*) Six and a half percent.
cent.

AURELIA. I was willing to take the whole mortgage at *three* percent, but—

SYLVIA. (*Quickly.*) And now you will have a lovely country house to visit next summer! Thanks so much. Lots of love, Sivvy.

AURELIA. (*Amused, admiring; they did it anyway!*) Devon, England, September 4, 1961

SYLVIA. Dear Mother, We moved without mishap on Thursday and had a fine, hot, sunny, blue day for it. Ever since, a fog has shrouded us in; just as well, for we have been unpacking, scrubbing, painting and working hard. The place is like a person; it responds to the slightest touch and looks wonderful immediately. My whole spirit has expanded. This is a wonderful place to have babies!

AURELIA. (*Cautioning.*) Ted has been driving thirty-five miles to the BBC . . . Ted had a day in London this Tuesday . . .

SYLVIA. Ted woke up this morning and said, "I dreamed you won a twenty-five dollar prize for your story about Johnny Panic." Well, I went downstairs and found out I had won a Saxton grant for two thousand dollars!

AURELIA. Today came a big Christmas parcel from you with the two *Ladies Home Journal* magazines.

SYLVIA. I love it! Recipes in English magazines are for things like "Lard and Stale Bread Pie, garnished with Cold Pigs Feet," or "Left-Over Pot Roast in Aspic."
AURELIA. I feel so thwarted not to be giving out anything but cards, but we really need to pinch this year to weather the piles of bills for plumbers, electricians, extra heaters, coal, land tax, house tax, solicitors, surveyors, movers . . .
SYLVIA. Small things loom very large.
AURELIA. Oh, saw my doctor. I look forward to my home delivery. Given up all pretence of working in my study. I am simply too ponderous.
SYLVIA. Dear Mother, By now I hope you have received the telegram Ted sent.
AURELIA. Our first son, Nicholas Farrar Hughes . . .
SYLVIA. All during the delivery, I felt it would be a boy. Then at five minutes to twelve, as the doctor was on his way over—this great bluish, glistening boy shot out onto the bed in a tidal wave of water that drenched all of us to the skin, howling lustily! It was an amazing sight. I immediately sat up and felt wonderful—no tears, nothing.
AURELIA. Now everything is quiet and peaceful. Ted is heating the apple pie I made to tide us over.
SYLVIA. Oh, how I look forward to your visit! I long to have a day or two on jaunts with just Ted. We can hardly see each other over the mountains of diapers and demands of babies. Tell Warren to get a big house with a soundproof bedroom before *he* has a baby. I am so longing for spring! (SYLVIA *begins to sing softly.*)
AURELIA. The ecstasy that followed the birth of Nicholas . . .
SYLVIA. (*Singing.*) His eyes are a deep slate-blue . . .
AURELIA. and the blooming of their gardens after the long harsh winter . . .
SYLVIA. Our daffodils and jonquils are wonderful. I have such spring fever, don't want to see another dish or cook another meal! I am dying for you to come, to see it all through your eyes. I have got awfully homesick for you since the last baby . . . All through this, I've not said anything about Warren's engagement. How wonderful! What fun for you to have all the traditional trappings for *one* of your children—diamond ring, Bachrach, a formal wedding—
AURELIA. I am now awaiting Ted's return from a daytrip to London.
SYLVIA. Having babies is really the happiest experience of my life. I would just like to go on and on. I have the queerest feeling of having been reborn with Frieda, as if my real, rich, happy life only started about then. I feel I'm just beginning at writing, too! Well, I must get supper for my family. Lots of love from us all. Sivvy.
AURELIA. By June . . .
SYLVIA. Honestly, the reason I have been so slow in writing is that I have said to myself, "I will write tomorrow; then it is sure to be a sunny day and how cheerful I will be." Believe it or not, we haven't seen the sun for *three weeks*. I have been feeling tired . . . hope the Strontium 90 level doesn't go up too high in milk . . . been very gloomy about the bomb news . . . got awfully depressed reading about the terrifying marriage of big business and the military in America, the John Birch Society, etc. . . . I seem to need sleep all the time . . . the day a whirlwind of baths, laundry, meals, feedings, and . . .
AURELIA. (*Overlap.*) The marriage
SYLVIA. (*Overlap.*) I am the busiest and happiest—! My book is due out! Our daffodils and jonquils—! Lots of love to you all.
AURELIA. The welcome I received when I arrived in June was heartwarming.
SYLVIA. This is the fourth day in a row of absolutely halcyon, blue, clean, hot weather. I have such lovely children and such a lovely home now!
AURELIA. After the first few days, I sensed a tension between Sylvia and Ted.
SYLVIA. Honestly, the *reason*—
AURELIA. On July 9th Sylvia said proudly, "I have everything in life I ever wanted: a wonderful husband, two adorable children, a lovely home"
SYLVIA. "and my writing."
AURELIA. Yet the marriage was—

ACT II LETTERS HOME 31

SYLVIA. No!
AURELIA. the marriage was seriously troubled Ted had been seeing someone else and Sylvia's jealousy was very intense. I thought it best to leave.

SYLVIA. No!
Never . . . seeing.

Never speak to God again!

Leave!

(*Low.*) On August 4, 1962, the four of them were together, waiting for my train to pull out of the station. The two parents were watching me stonily. Nick was the only one with a smile. (*She turns away.*) It was the last time I saw Sylvia.

SYLVIA. (*Flat, calm now.*) August 27, 1962
I do not believe in divorce.
Dear Mother, I hope you will not be too surprised or shocked when I say I am going to try to get a legal separation from Ted. I have too much at stake and am too rich a person to live as a martyr. I want a clean break, so I can breathe and laugh and enjoy myself again. Tell no one but perhaps Margaret and Warren of this, perhaps not even them. It is a private matter and I do not want people who would never see me anyway to know of it. I am in need of nothing and desirous of nothing! I meant you to have such a lovely stay!
September 23, 1962
I will try to rent the house and live in the cottage. I want to be where no possessions remind me of the past and by the sea, which is for me the great healer. I must at all costs get a live-in nanny, so I can start to write and get my independence again.
    AURELIA. (*Eagerly.*) September 24, 1962
I begin to see that life is not over for me! It is the uncertainty, week after week, that has been such a torture. And, of course, the desire to hang on to the last to see if something, anything, could be salvaged.
    SYLVIA. It is a beautiful day here, clear and blue . . .
    AURELIA. I got this nanny back for today and tomorrow, a whiz, and I see what heaven my life could be if I had a good live-in nanny!
    SYLVIA. I will rent the house for the winter and go to Ireland. I dream of Warren and Maggie! I would love to go on a skiing holiday in the Tyrol with them someday. I just read about it in the paper. And then if I do a novel or two, I might apply for a Guggenheim to go to Rome with the children. Right now I have no money, but if I get the cottage done this winter—
    AURELIA. I might even take a London flat, send the children to the fine free schools there and enjoy the London people.
    SYLVIA. I went up to London to the solicitor yesterday. The laws are awful! A wife is allowed one third of her husband's income, and if he doesn't pay up, the suing is long and costly. Together we earned a fine salary, I earning one third. Now it is all gone. I shall be penalized for earning, or, if I don't earn, have to beg. Well I choose to invest everything with courage in the cottage and the nanny and *write like mad*. I must get control of my life!
    AURELIA. It is the evenings here that are the worst . . .
    SYLVIA. I do have to take sleeping pills, but they are, just now, a necessary evil.
    AURELIA. I have to get a nanny in the spring. I don't break down with someone else around!
    SYLVIA. Dear Mother, I don't know where to begin. I just can't take the $50!
    AURELIA. I finally persuaded her to do so, monthly, and opened a joint account in a London bank, so she could use it in any emergency—hoping she would consider returning to the United States. We, as a family, were prepared to set her up in her own apartment here.

SYLVIA. America is out for me! If I start running now, I will never stop. I shall hear of Ted all my life, of his success, his genius. I must make a life all my own as fast as I can! The flesh has dropped from my bones. But I am a fighter! I want a flat in London. The cultural life is what I am starved for! . . . I haven't the strength to see you for some time. The horror of what you saw—

AURELIA. (*Anguished.*) what I *saw* you see—

SYLVIA. is between us, and I cannot face you again until I have a new life; it would be too great a strain. I was very stupid, very happy . . . no time to make any plans of my own. I have *no one*. Stuck down here as into a sack, I fight for air and freedom. I will need protection. I look to Warren now that I have no man, no adviser. Everything is breaking!—my dinner set cracking in half, the health inspector says the cottage should be demolished—there is no hope for it. Even my beloved bees set upon me today when I knocked aside their sugar feeder, and I am all over stings! If I can spend the winter in the sun in Spain . . . Spain is out of the question! I could take the children to Ireland. I must get to London next fall! *Please* tell Warren to say he and Maggie will come in spring! In Ireland I may find my soul, and in London my brain, and maybe in heaven what was my heart. Love, S.

AURELIA. These letters were, of course, written under great strain. They are desperate letters, and their very desperation make it difficult to read them with any objectivity. I could not, at the time. Dear Mother, I have had an incredible change in spirit; I am joyous, happier than I have been for ages. My life can begin. Every morning, when my sleeping pill wears off, I am up about five, in my study with coffee, writing like mad—a poem a day before breakfast. Terrific stuff, as if domesticity had choked me. I need a bloody holiday. I miss *brains*, hate this cow life, am dying to surround myself with intelligent, good people. I am a famous poetess here—mentioned this week in *The Listener* as one of the half-dozen women who will last.

SYLVIA. Dearest Warren and Maggie, I have been through the most incredible hell for six months, and, amazingly enough,

AURELIA. the one thing I retain is love and admiration of Ted's writing. He is a genius, and for a genius there are no bonds and no bounds. It is hurtful to be ditched, but thank God I have my own work.

SYLVIA. I think I'll be a pretty good novelist. My stuff makes me laugh and laugh, and if I can laugh now it must be hellishly funny! Just now I am a bit of a wreck, bones literally sticking out all over and great black shadows under my eyes from sleeping pills, a smoker's hack (I actually took up smoking the past month out of desperation and I practically burned off all my eyebrows!) Tell me you'll consider taking me (I mean escorting; I'll have money!) to Austria with you, even if you don't, so I'll have that to look forward to. I've had nothing to look forward to for so long!

AURELIA. Dear Mother, I am writing with my old fever of 101° alternating with chills. I need help very much just now. Home is impossible! I can go nowhere with the children, and I am ill, and it would be psychologically the worst thing to see you now. I am a writer. I am a genius of a writer. I am writing the best poems of my life. They will make my name.

SYLVIA. Very bad luck with nanny agency; a bitch of a woman is coming tomorrow from them; doesn't want to cook, do any breakfast or tea, wondered if there was a butler—? Ten pounds a week! If I had time to get a good nanny, I could get on with my life! *I am all right.* Could either Dot or Margaret spare me six weeks? I must have someone I love to protect me. The babes are beautiful—though Frieda has regressed. *I cannot come home.* I am full of plans, but do need help for the next two months. I am fighting now against hard odds, and alone. Mention has been made of my coming home for Christmas. Do you suppose instead

AURELIA. (*Low.*) Fighting now . . .

there is any possibility of your chipping in and sending me Maggie? Could she come *now* instead of then? I already love her; she would be such *fun* and love the babies. Do I sound mad? Taking or wanting to take Warren's new wife? Just for a few weeks! I need someone from *home*. A defender. I have a fever now, so I am a bit delirious. I work from four to eight a.m. On the next few months depend my future and my health. I am fine in mind and spirit, but wasted and ill in flesh. I love you all. Sivvy.

AURELIA. On receiving the above letter, I cabled Mrs. Winifred Davies, Sylvia's midwife and friend: "Please see Sylvia now and get woman for her! *Salary paid here!*"

SYLVIA. Winifred, bless her, came round last night with some hopeful news! A young nurse nearby would love to live in till mid-December! The weather has been heavenly—fog mornings, but clear, sunny, blue days after. I have a bad cough and shall get my lungs x-rayed and my teeth seen to. I am writing very good poems. I need time to breathe, sun, recover my flesh. I love and live for letters. Dear Warren, I know what I need, want, must work for. *Please* convince mother of this. She identifies much too much with me, and you must help her see how starting my own life in the most difficult place, here—not running, is the only sane thing to do. I wrote two worrying letters when I was desperate. Do try to convince mother I am cured. I am a writer and that is all I want to do; have had my first novel accepted (a pot-boiler and no one must read it!) Don't tell mother! Dear Mother, Will you please, for goodness sake, stop bothering poor Winifred Davies! She is busier than either you or I, and knows and sees my situation much better than you can. She came over this afternoon and said you sent her some wire? Please do understand that while I am very very grateful indeed for financial help from people who *have* money, I want no monthly dole, especially not from you. You can help me best by saving your money for your own retirement. I am doing a poem a morning, great things. Don't talk to me about the world needing cheerful stuff! What the person out of Belsen wants is nobody saying the birdies still go tweet-tweet, but the full knowledge that somebody else has been there and knows the *worst*. It is much more help for me to know that people are divorced and go through hell, than to hear about

AURELIA. Fighting . . .

AURELIA. against hard odds . . . fighting, fighting . . .

AURELIA. (*In anguish.*) "fighting . . . alone"

happy marriages. Let the *Ladies' Home Journal* blither about *those*. I know just what I want and want to do. I am well liked here, in spite of my weirdness, I think. I adore the babies and am glad to have them, even though they make life fantastically difficult now. The worst is that Ted is at the peak of his fame and all his friends—But I can manage that, too. Dear Mother, *Please* forgive my grumpy, sick letters.

(*In the form of a "round".*)

... I see now just what I need*, not professional nannies who are snotty and expensive, but an adventurous, young, cheerful girl to whom my life would be *fun*. O, it is *ideal*! ... I must be one of the most creative people in the world! I must get back to the live, lively, always learning and developing person I was! I want to study, learn history, politics, languages, travel. I want to be the most loving and fascinating mother in the world—and I shall, in spite of all obstacles, have that, and Frieda and Nick and the Salon I deserve. I shall be a *rich, active woman!*

AURELIA. ... *I see now just what I need, not professional nannies who are snotty and expensive, but an adventurous, young, cheerful girl to whom my life would be *fun*. O, it is *ideal*! ... I must be one of the most creative people in the world! I must get back to the live, lively, always learning and developing person I was! I want to study, learn history, politics, languages, travel. I want to be the most loving and fascinating mother in the world—and I shall, in spite of all obstacles, have that, and Frieda and Nick and the Salon I deserve. I shall be a rich, active woman!

(SYLVIA *hears how all this sounds to* AURELIA.)

SYLVIA. (*Softer.*) I should love to use your birthday check on a dress. I shall take all my hems up. All my clothes are ten years old! Just wait till I hit London! Dearest Warren and Maggie, The critic of the *Observer* says I'm the first woman poet he's taken seriously since Emily Dickinson! Now can you possibly get mother to stop worrying so much? Dear Mother, Now *stop* trying to get me to write about "decent courageous people"! Read the *Ladies Home Journal* for those! I believe in going through and facing the worst, not hiding from it. That is why I am going to London this week—to face all the people we know and tell them happily and squarely I am divorcing Ted, so they won't picture me as a poor country wife. I am not going to steer clear of these professional acquaintances just because they know or because I may meet Ted with someone else. Dear Mother, I am writing from London, so happy I can hardly speak. I have a place! By an absolute *fluke* the street and the house where I've always wanted to live. Flew to the agents. It seems I have a chance! And guess what—it is *Yeats' house*, with a blue plaque over the door, saying *he lived* there! I am now staying with a wonderful Portuguese couple, the girl a friend of Ted's girl, and they see how I am, full of

AURELIA. (*Softly.*) "Love ...
Sylvia ... Sivvy ... Cyrilly ...
Your maturing ...
crazy old ...

happy ...

dearest ...

interest in my own life, and are amazed, as everyone is, at my complete lack of jealousy or sorrow. I have found a *fabulous* hairdresser, and the cut, shampoo and set was only $1.50. I did it on your cheque. Men stare at me in the street now, truck drivers whistle, it's amazing. Living apart from Ted is wonderful— I am no longer in his shadow . . . it is heaven to be liked for myself alone . . . I may even borrow a table for my flat from Ted's girl. I could be gracious to her now . . . She has only her high-paid job, her vanity . . . and *everybody* wants to be a writer. I may be poor in bank funds, but I am so much richer in every other way, I envy them nothing. My babies and my writing are my life! Wish me luck. Sivvy.

whom I love better than anybody . . ."

AURELIA. The most, the absolute,

love, I am so happy,

singing,

O he has everything! Sivvy.

(*It is very hard for* AURELIA *to go on.*)

AURELIA. In December she closed the large house in Devon and moved with the children to a flat in Yeat's former home in London, where, for a brief time, she responded excitedly to the cultural stimulation of the city. Then the worst cold, snowstorms, and blackouts in over a hundred years engulfed London for months. Sylvia fought off flu; the children had coughs and colds. In spite of all this, she continued the writing she had started in Devon. She began at 7 a.m. each morning to pour forth magnificently structured poems, renouncing the subservient female role, yet holding to the triumphant note of maternal creativity in her scorn of "barrenness." Feeling she needed a backlog of funds to prepare for the sterile periods every writer dreads, she had earlier sent out *The Bell Jar*, under a pseudonym, in the firm belief that this would fully protect her from disclosure. By the time the novel appeared in London bookstores, she was ill, exhausted, and overwhelmed by the responsibilities she had to shoulder *alone*.

SYLVIA. Dear Mother, Well, here I am! Safely in Yeats' house! And I can truly say I have never been so happy in my life. I just sit thinking, shall I write a poem, shall I paint a floor, shall I hug a baby? Everything is such fun, such an adventure, and if I feel this way *now*, with everything bare and to be painted—

AURELIA. "What will the green young spring be like? . . ."

SYLVIA. (*Disjointed.*) . . . Clear, crisp blue day . . . I arrived here to find no gas stove in and no electricity connected! . . . first letter

SYLVIA. Someone to love me . . .

to be with me at night . . .

. . . the cement tunnels leading down to the shock room . . .

AURELIA. The green young . . .

through my door was from my publishers . . .
Oslo, Norway . . . to translate and do . . .
"Three Women" and A. Alvarez . . . best
poetry critic here, thinks my second book . . .
should win Pulitzer Prize . . . Everybody . . . spring . . .
says you worry if I don't write. For goodness
sake, remember no news is good news! Lots
and lots of love to all, Your happy Sivvy.

AURELIA. (*Slowly, painfully.*) I am in the best of hands. I am slowly pulling out of the flu, but the weakness and tiredness makes me cross.

SYLVIA. (*A new voice.*) The weather has been filthy . . . all the heaped snow freezing . . . the roads are narrow ruts, and I have been very gloomy with the long wait for a phone . . . which makes me feel cut off, along with the lack of an "au pair." I did interview a very nice German girl of eighteen . . . but her employer is making difficulties . . . Still need to sew the bedroom curtains, have some made for the big front room, get a stair carpet. It is so hard to get out to shop with the babies. I have never been so happy in my life.

AURELIA. Still have the babies' floors to paint, the "au pair's," the hall floors and three wood bureaus. *Blue* is my new color, royal, midnight (not aqua). Ted never liked blue.

SYLVIA. Oh, Mother . . .

AURELIA. My German "au pair" is food-fussy and boy-gaga, but she does give me some peace mornings. My solicitor is gathering evidence for a Divorce Petition.

SYLVIA. Your package came today.

AURELIA. There have been electric strikes and every so often the lights and heaters go out for hours; children freeze; dinners are stopped; there are mad rushes for candles . . .

SYLVIA. I am going to start seeing a woman doctor free on the National Health which should help me weather this difficult time. Don't worry about my paying bills. I pay them immediately. Always have. My love to all. Sylvia.

AURELIA. On February 12

SYLVIA. (*A cry.*) Oh, Mother!

AURELIA. (*Struggling to go on.*) 1963 . . .

SYLVIA. It is a blue, blue day, blue skied, leaves golden . . .

AURELIA. My sister received a cablegram from Ted, telling us Sylvia died yesterday. SYLVIA. falling . . .

SYLVIA. And life is good.

AURELIA. (*Her whole soul naked.*) "*I'll never speak to God—*"

SYLVIA. *No!* A moment, then:

AURELIA. No. . .

SYLVIA. (*More softly.*) No.

AURELIA. (*A decision. To herself, to Sylvia, to the audience; gathering resolution, strength.*)
November 13, 1949
As of today I have decided to keep a diary again—just a place where I can write my thoughts and opinions when I have a moment. Somehow I have to keep and hold the rapture of being *seventeen*. Every day is so precious. I feel infinitely sad at the thought of all this time melting farther and farther away from me as I grow older. *Now, now* is the perfect time of my life. I still do not know myself. Perhaps I never will. But I feel free—unbound by responsibility, I still can come up to my own private room,

with my drawings hanging on the walls, and pictures pinned up over my bureau—a room suited to me, uncluttered and peaceful. I love the quiet lines of the furniture, the two bookcases filled with poetry books and fairy tales saved from childhood. Always I want to be an observer. I want to be affected by life deeply, but never so blinded that I cannot see my share of existence in a wry, humorous light . . . I am afraid of getting older. I am afraid of getting married. Spare me from cooking three meals a day—spare me from the relentless cage of routine and rote. I want to be *free*—free to know people and their backgrounds—free to move to different parts of the world. I want, I think, to be omniscient. I think I would like to call myself "the girl who wanted to be God" . . . Perhaps I am *destined* to be classified and qualified. But, oh, I cry out against it. I am I. I love my flesh, my face, my limbs. I have erected in my mind an image of myself, idealistic and beautiful. Is not that image, free from blemish, the true self—the true perfection? (Oh, even now I glance back on what I have just written—how foolish it sounds, how overdramatic!) Never, never, never will I reach the perfection I long for with all my soul. There will come a time when I must face myself at last. Even now I dread the big choices which loom up in my life. I am afraid. I feel uncertain. I am not as wise as I have thought. I can now see, as from a valley, the roads lying open for me, but I cannot see the end—the consequences. Oh, I love *now*, with all my fears and forebodings, for now I still am not completely molded. *I am strong.* My life is still just beginning!

SYLVIA. (*Very softly.*) A certain color in . . . the sea

Blue

love
the busiest

happiest
sharing girl in the
It is an Indian summer day
I feel that I am . . .

. . . learning.

BLACKOUT

PROPERTY PLOT

Stage Left Bookcase: (Sylvia's)
Top Shelf: (from SR to SL)
        Kid's mug (handle turned SR)
        Kid's mug (handle turned SL)
        Picture of Ted and Sylvia in standing gold frame
        Book of Ted's poetry
        8 books

Second: Composition book
        Record book (on top of composition book)
        Writing tablet (on top of record book)
        Spiral notebook
        3 pencils
        Hair brush
        Book with Sylvia's letter
        8 books

Third: 2 lunch sized plates stacked; breakable one on top.
        2 sets of silverware on two white napkins.
        green glass vase
        Bunch of white mums; stems upstage
        spool of blue thread
        Child's nightgown with threaded needle inserted in hem.
        Dish rag
        Table scarf

Bottom: 6 large books
        2 teacups on saucers (DS)
        teapot (US)
        Folded man's shirt

Stage Right Bookcase: (Aurelia's)
Top Shelf: (From SR to SL)
        Silver teapot
        Silver creamer
        Floral plate in stand

Second: Copy of Sylvia's drawing in standing frame
        Clip on earrings in small box
        Bud vase with fake flowers
        Sylvia's diary
        7 books

Third: 6 books
        Picture of Sylvia and Warren in standing frame
        Silver sugar bowl

PROPERTY PLOT

Bottom: 3 pillows

On Table: Sketch pad
Sylvia's drawing
Drawing pencil

On sofa: One pillow (SR)
Afghan thrown on back

COSTUME PLOT

SYLVIA.
Act I: Green V Necked Sweater
        White blouse (over sweater)
        Tweed skirt
        tan hose
        blue pumps

Act II: Same as Act I except for brown pumps

AURELIA.
Act I and II: Rose blouse
        Rose plaid skirt and jacket
        gold stick pin in lapel
        pearl earrings
        tan hose
        black shoes with low heel
        gray wig

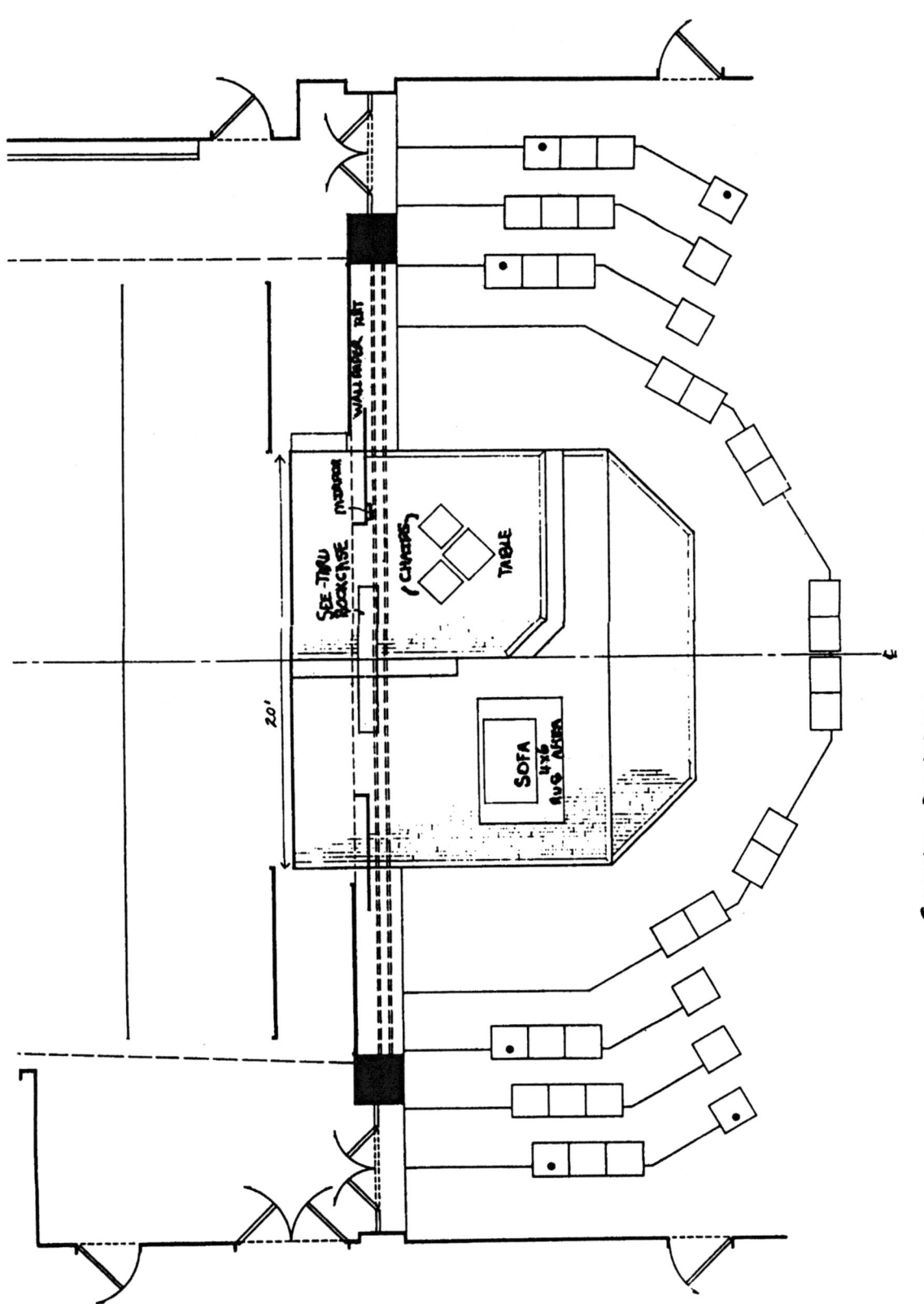

SCENE DESIGN: LETTERS HOME